In Essentials, Unity

New Approaches to Midwestern Studies
SERIES EDITORS: PAUL FINKELMAN AND L. DIANE BARNES

Nikki M. Taylor, *Driven toward Madness: The Fugitive Slave Margaret Garner and Tragedy on the Ohio*

Jenny Bourne, *In Essentials, Unity: An Economic History of the Grange Movement*

An Economic History of the Grange Movement

JENNY BOURNE

Ohio University Press   Athens

Ohio University Press, Athens, Ohio 45701
ohioswallow.com
© 2017 by Ohio University Press
All rights reserved

To obtain permission to quote, reprint, or otherwise reproduce or distribute material from Ohio University Press publications, please contact our rights and permissions department at (740) 593-1154 or (740) 593-4536 (fax).

Printed in the United States of America
Ohio University Press books are printed on acid-free paper ∞ ™
27 26 25 24 23 22 21 20 19 18 17   5 4 3 2 1

Library of Congress Cataloging-in-Publication Data
available upon request.

Hardcover ISBN 978-0-8214-2236-6
Paperback ISBN 978-0-8214-2237-3
eISBN 978-0-8214-4581-5

book supported by

Figure Foundation

progress with truth

For Austin,

Jackson,

and my kin at

Thomas Farms

Contents

List of Illustrations xi

Series Editors' Preface xiii

Acknowledgments xvii

Introduction 1

1 "Our Agricultural Brotherhood"
  Origins, Purposes, and Structure 5

2 The Granger Railroad Laws 31

3 The Grange's Ambitious Experiments with Private Cooperation 45

4 The Grange as a Fraternal, Educational, and Charitable Organization
  The Minnehaha Grange as a Case Study 67

5 Legacies of the Grange
  Its Influence on Grassroots Organizations and American Law 93

Notes 109

References 123

Index 133

Illustrations

Figures

1.1. Grangers versus Grasshoppers, 1880 7
1.2. Oliver Kelley, 1875 8
1.3. Grange Membership, 1875–1960 10
1.4. Oliver Kelley Farm, 2013 11
1.5. Minnehaha Grange Hall, 1945 13
1.6. Minnehaha Grange Hall, 2013 13
1.7. Grange Badge, 1867 15
1.8. Officers of the Minnehaha Grange, 1944–45 15
1.9. Degree Tableaux, 1947 16
1.10. Organizational Structure of the Grange 17
1.11. Midwestern Farm Prices and Consumer Price Index, 1870–1900 21
1.12. Farm and Economy-Wide Productivity, 1800–1900 21
1.13. Density of Minnesota Granges by County and Minnesota Railroad Lines, 1874 26
2.1. First Locomotive into St. Peter, Minnesota, 1870 36
3.1. Ignatius Donnelly, 1880 47
3.2. Regional Proportions of Grange Families, 1875–1960 51
3.3. Farm Organization Membership, 1874–1933 56
3.4. Farm Organization Membership, 1936–84 56
3.5. Membership Reported to Minnesota State Grange, 1881–1916 62
3.6. Percent Change in Grange Membership and Real Per Capita Farm Income, 1917–30 63
3.7. Establishment of Newly Organized Minnesota Granges by County, 1900–1970 65
4.1. First Worthy Master James A. Bull, Minnehaha Grange 69
4.2. Monument to Caroline Hall, Lakewood Cemetery, Minneapolis 71

4.3. Lumberjack Night, 1948 75
4.4. Minnehaha Grange State Fair Booth, 1948 78
4.5. Parade Float, Minnehaha Grange, 1947 89
4.6. Ladies' Nail-Driving Contest, 1947 90
4.7. Men's Needle-Threading Contest, 1947 91

Table

1.1. Farm Number, Size, and Value, 1850–80 28

Series Editors' Preface

For much of American history the term "Midwest" evoked images of endless fields of grain, flat, treeless landscapes, and homogenized populations in small towns. Most Americans hear "Midwest" and think of corn, wheat, soybeans, massive feedlots, huge pig farms, and countless dairy herds. The cinematic Midwest was River City, Iowa, in *The Music Man*; Dorothy trying to escape Oz and get back to Kansas; the iconic power of small-town basketball portrayed in *Hoosiers*; or a mythical baseball diamond in rural Iowa in *Field of Dreams*. In the late twentieth century, images of deindustrialization and decay linked the region to a new identity as the nation's Rust Belt. For too many Americans, the Midwest has been "flyover country."

This book series explores regional identity in the nation's past through the lens of the American Midwest. Stereotypical images of the region ignore the complexity and vibrancy of the region, as well as the vital role it has played—and continues to play—in the nation's economy, politics, and social history. In the antebellum and Civil War periods the Midwest was home to virulent racist opponents of black rights and black migration but also to a vibrant antislavery movement, the vigorous and often successful Underground Railroad, and the political and military leadership that brought an end to slavery and reframed the Constitution to provide at least formal racial equality. A midwestern president issued the Emancipation Proclamation, and midwestern generals led the armies that defeated the southern slaveocracy. Midwestern politicians authored the Thirteenth Amendment ending slavery and the Fourteenth Amendment mandating legal equality for all Americans. The political impact of the region is exemplified by the fact that from 1860 to 1932 only two elected presidents (Grover Cleveland and Woodrow Wilson) were not from the Midwest. Significantly, from 1864 until the 1930s every Chief Justice but one was also a midwesterner.

While many Americans imagine the region as one of small towns and farms, the Midwest was the home to major urban centers. In 1920 three of the five largest cities in the nation were in the Midwest, and even today, despite massive migration to the sunbelt, there are four midwestern cities in the top fifteen. The great urban centers of the Midwest include Chicago, Detroit, Cincinnati, Cleveland, Columbus, Indianapolis, Milwaukee, Minneapolis, St. Louis, and Kansas City. For a century—from the late nineteenth century to the late twentieth century—the region was not only an agricultural heartland but also the nation's industrial heartland. Many of the key industries of the twentieth century began in the Midwest and developed there. Many midwestern cities were known by the industries they dominated, such as Detroit (automobiles), Toledo (glass), Akron (rubber), flour and milling (Minneapolis), and even breakfast cereals (Battle Creek). While most Americans associate the oil industry with Texas and Oklahoma, it began with John D. Rockefeller's Standard Oil Company in Cleveland. The airplane industry began with the Wright Brothers in Ohio and with the manufacturing of planes in Wichita. While Pittsburgh (which was almost a midwestern city) called itself the "steel city," more steel was manufactured in Youngstown, Gary, Chicago, Cleveland, and other midwestern cities, usually from ore that came from Minnesota's Iron Range. The Midwest was always America's agricultural heartland, producing grains, pork, beef, and dairy products. But this food production led to midwestern industries beyond the farms. Beef and pork raised in the Midwest were processed and packaged in Cincinnati in the antebellum period, and later in Chicago and other cities. Midwestern farmers and food processors fed the nation at lunch and dinner, while General Mills, Kellogg, and Quaker Oats, complemented by bacon from Swift, Armor, and Hormel, provided breakfast for the nation. The cows and hogs that fed the nation were themselves fed by midwestern feed companies, while the crops were cultivated and harvested using machines built by International Harvester, John Deere, Massey-Ferguson, and similar companies.

All of these products were grown, processed, and manufactured by migrants from the East and the South, and immigrants mostly from Central, Eastern, and Southern Europe and the Ottoman Empire. The Midwest of the popular imagination was homogeneous and almost boring; in reality the Midwest that emerged in the early twentieth century was as culturally, ethnically, racially, and religiously diverse as it was economically diverse.

The books in this series capture the complexity of the Midwest and its historical and continuing role in the development of modern America.

Jenny Bourne's study of the Granger Movement illuminates much about the Midwest and its role in the nation. The movement came out of America's heartland, as farmers in post–Civil War America felt squeezed by large economic forces, powerful railroads, and other industries (such as those manufacturing tractors and other farm equipment). Railroads, large processing companies, and middlemen controlled the cost of moving goods to market—but the farmers themselves had little power to respond to these powerful entities. The Granger Movement was an attempt by farmers to level the playing field through collective cooperation, voting, and legislation. As Professor Bourne teaches us in this book, sometimes the movement succeeded, but often it failed. Beyond the economic factors, however, the movement also provided education, opportunities for knowledge, and camaraderie among midwestern farmers that helped sustain them in many ways, while sometimes also improving midwesterners' economic circumstances.

Paul Finkelman
L. Diane Barnes

Acknowledgments

Many thanks to Carleton colleagues: Nathan Grawe for his unstinting encouragement and friendship, Mark Kanazawa for his expertise on Illinois law, and Aaron Swoboda for his invaluable help in preparing the maps. I am grateful to Gillian Berchowitz, L. Diane Barnes, Nancy Basmajian, and Teresa Jesionowski for editorial advice, the staff at the Minnesota Historical Society for obtaining material and providing a welcoming atmosphere, and T. J. Malaskee for conversations about the present-day Grange. Special thanks to Austin Wahl for constructive criticism and superb photography, and to Jackson Wahl for pithy observations on what to include in graphs and text (and, more important, what to omit). I am indebted most of all to Paul Finkelman, whose support, kindness, and generosity are beyond measure.

Introduction

> United by the strong and faithful tie of Agriculture, we mutually resolve to labor for the good of our order, our country, and mankind. We heartily [e]ndorse the motto, "In essentials, unity; in non-essentials, liberty; in all things, charity."
>
> —*Declaration of Purposes of the Patrons of Husbandry*[1]

The Carrabelle and Thomasville Railroad Company received its corporate charter on 17 February 1881. A new railroad proposed at this time in US history was not surprising: total rail mileage across the reunified nation more than doubled in the ten years after the Civil War and would nearly double again in the following decade.[2] But one name on this particular charter—Oliver Hudson Kelley—is startling. In 1867, Kelley had founded the Patrons of Husbandry, also known as the Grange, a group centered primarily in the Midwest and best known for its association with Gilded-Age laws aimed at curbing the monopoly power of railroads.

Kelley's involvement with the Carrabelle and Thomasville highlights the complex, ambivalent relationship between traditional agriculture and modern modes of business and transportation. The Grange movement itself constitutes a major episode in American economic history; the Grange organization made its mark on American legal history as well. Its crucial center in the Midwest helps us understand the importance of that region to the development of the US economy and US jurisprudence in the latter half of the nineteenth century and the first half of the twentieth. This book also explores a fascinating slice of social history from the American Midwest via a century of records left by a local Minnesota chapter of the Grange.

The heyday of the Patrons of Husbandry came just after the Civil War. Chapter 1 explores their origins, stated purposes, and structure. The war and its aftermath exacted a toll on small farmers, leaving them ripe for an organization that took their interests to heart. Fees charged by middlemen and railroads seemed particularly oppressive, and frequent financial upheavals throughout the nineteenth and early twentieth centuries created considerable anxiety for rural households. Oliver Kelley's vision of agricultural collaboration seemed providential to isolated, indebted smallholders.

Improving the economic status of farmers via collective action was the heart of the Grange's original mission. Kelley was an indefatigable organizer; his Masonic background helped shape the Grange's rituals and hierarchical form. Kelley's fondness for his niece Caroline Arabella Hall led to the nearly unheard-of inclusion of women in the association, as well as inspired the name of his railroad. Bylaws required each local chapter of the Grange to include at least one-third female enrollment. By 1875, the Grange boasted close to a million members, nearly half of them in the Midwest.

Tensions among competing economic factions gave rise to the so-called "Granger railroad laws"; chapter 2 investigates this legislation and case law. Statutes passed in four Midwestern states in the late 1870s launched a new role for government in regulating private industry. Subsequent lawsuits—most notably *Munn v. Illinois*[3]—were the first to invoke the due process clause of the newly ratified Fourteenth Amendment to the US Constitution. These "Granger cases" formed the foundation for modern transport regulation as well as provided key precedents for government intervention in privately held enterprises that were "clothed with a public interest." Although the Granger laws themselves were short-lived, they left a significant imprint on US jurisprudence.

Self-sufficiency and disdain for the middleman led the Patrons of Husbandry to undertake a variety of cooperative endeavors, including centralized purchasing, manufacturing, and sales. Chapter 3 looks at the early success and subsequent fizzling of most of these efforts, and the near demise of the organization itself. The remarkable explosion in the number of Grangers in the first half of the 1870s is matched by an equally precipitous decline in the second half. Organizations more politically active in representing agricultural interests—such as the Farmers' Alliance and the Greenback Party—emerged in importance, only to be supplanted later by the National Farmers' Union and the Farm Bureau. The enormous success of the Farm Bureau stemmed in part from its association with farm extension programs in land-grant colleges, which are supported chiefly by public funding.

Although the Grange formed primarily for economic reasons, its early members also emphasized a commitment to education, community service, and fraternalism. After 1879, these features kept the Patrons alive. Unlike other nineteenth-century farmers' organizations, the Grange continues to the present day and prides itself on being the longest-lived American agricultural society.[4] Chapter 4 draws heavily on a new data source—the minute books and other materials from the Minnehaha Grange (Minnesota No. 398)—to present a lively picture of the inner workings of one of longest-lasting local Granges in the nation.

The Minnehaha met twice monthly between September and May from its founding in 1873 to its last official gathering in 1978. In 1880, it built its own hall, which still stands in the Minneapolis suburb of Edina, Minnesota. The chapter concerned itself with a wide range of issues, including gender equity at the University of Minnesota, the safety of electrical appliances, the suspect nature of oleomargarine, the admission of China to the United Nations, and the size of portions in local restaurants. In 1894, Sarah Baird of the Minnehaha became the first female ever to head a state Grange. For years, the women of the Minnehaha tended the grave of Caroline Hall in Minneapolis's Lakewood Cemetery.

The final chapter of this book considers the legacies left by the Patrons of Husbandry. The early Granger efforts show how collective action can succeed when aspirations and talents are well matched, and how it can fail when they are not. These failures convinced even doubters that middlemen can serve a useful function and that specialization and comparative advantage are powerful economic concepts.

Yet the issues raised by Oliver Kelley and his followers remain fresh: What does "clothed with a public interest" mean? How do we interpret the due process clause? And what is the role of the government in regulating private behavior? Citations to the famous

Introduction

Granger case of *Munn v. Illinois* appear in landmark Supreme Court opinions on topics ranging from minimum wage, rent control, and environmental regulation to birth control and lunch-counter sit-ins. Some scholars consider the Granger laws as a foundation for the Sherman Act and other antitrust statutes. Echoes of the Granger movement reverberate still, from the Occupy Wall Street protest that began on Constitution Day 2011 to the controversy surrounding the Patient Protection and Affordable Care Act.[5] In short, the history of the Patrons of Husbandry exposes the classic tension between the desires for achieving overall economic success and for dictating how the spoils are split.

1

"Our Agricultural Brotherhood"

Origins, Purposes, and Structure

> We propose meeting together, talking together, working together, buying together, selling together, and in general acting together for our mutual protection and advancement. . . . Sectionalism is, and of right should be dead and buried with the past. . . . In our agricultural brotherhood . . . we shall recognize no North, no South, no East, no West.
>
> —*Declaration of Purposes of the Patrons of Husbandry*

Months before President Andrew Johnson formally declared an end to the US Civil War on 20 August 1866, he sent Bureau of Agriculture clerk Oliver Kelley to inspect the ravaged rural South. Six days after his fortieth birthday, Kelley departed Washington on 13 January 1866 and traveled across the South until 21 April, recording the effect of the war on southern agriculture.[1] Although the South bore the brunt of the war's devastation, farmers across the nation were suffering, especially when compared to the business titans emerging in the postbellum period.

A year and a half after Kelley's southern journey, the Patrons of Husbandry were born. The first official meeting of what became the Grange took place on 15 November 1867 in Washington, DC, and officers were elected on 4 December 1867. By no means the first nor the only American agricultural organization, the Grange nevertheless stands out for its longevity.[2] Improving the economic lot of farmers was its original focus, but the Grange has sustained itself primarily by its appeal as a fraternal and social association that engages in community service and political advocacy for farmers.

Setting the Stage for Farmer Discontent: Aftermath of the War

Military deaths during the Civil War accounted for more than 2 percent of the US population, with most of the dead being able-bodied men in their prime. An estimated one out of ten men of military age never returned home; nearly a quarter of Southern men ages twenty to twenty-four in 1860 lost their lives in the war. The demobilization of both armies sent hundreds of thousands of survivors back to their farms, but many of them returned to neglect and disarray. The men themselves did not always come back whole: for instance, 20 percent of Mississippi's entire state budget in 1866 went for artificial limbs. Although the Homestead Act of 1862 had opened up cheap land to aspiring farmers, improved capital-intensive farm technology made it difficult for small farmers to achieve economic success. Tumultuous weather and periodic pest infestations (fig. 1.1)—described so vividly in Laura Ingalls Wilder's *Little House* books—added to the misery.[3]

The official cessation of conflict also meant a downturn in demand for rations, animal feed, wool, horses, and mules. Emancipation and Reconstruction generated major changes in agricultural supply as well. Former slaves met with resistance, political suppression, and violence as they sought to distance themselves from the plantation and to grow their own crops and food. The war was over, but the struggle to move from a slave to a free society had only just begun. Under the leadership of General O. O. Howard, the Freedmen's Bureau made heroic efforts to smooth the transition, but lack of funds hampered the bureau, which was disbanded under President Ulysses S. Grant.

As a further irritant to farmers and other citizens, corruption plagued the postwar federal government. Perhaps the best-known episode was the Crédit Mobilier scandal, which consisted of financial

Grangers versus Grasshoppers, 1880. *Source:* Minnesota Historical Society

hijinks by the directors of the Union Pacific Railroad abetted by certain members of Congress. The public learned the details of Crédit Mobilier in 1872, during Grant's second run for office, but the shady behavior by government officials actually occurred during Andrew Johnson's administration.[4]

Financial turmoil and monetary policy took its toll on postbellum agriculture as well. Many farmers experienced setbacks during the massive financial panic of 1873. What is more, the nation's return to the gold standard after its experiment with greenbacks during the war meant precipitous price declines and financial uncertainty, which affected numerous farmers adversely.[5]

Even as farmers suffered, they observed others amassing enormous amounts of wealth. Extensive inequality existed in the United States throughout the nineteenth century, but it increased markedly between 1870 and the early twentieth century.[6] Some of the richest men in American history built their fortunes starting during this time, including John D. Rockefeller, Cornelius Vanderbilt, and Andrew Carnegie. Mark Twain and Charles Dudley Warner satirized the greed of this period—and bestowed its name—in 1873 in their coauthored book, *The Gilded Age: A Tale of Today.*

In short, the time was ripe for farmers to find an outlet to express their discontent. The Grange provided it.

Figure 1.2. Oliver Kelley, 1875. *Source:* Minnesota Historical Society

Oliver Kelley and the Founding of the Grange
Kelley's Early Years

Oliver Kelley (fig. 1.2) is generally acknowledged as the principal founder of the Grange, with his talent appearing to lie more in organizing than in actual farming. He grew up in Boston but moved to St. Paul in 1849, where he joined Minnesota's first Masonic Lodge. Kelley's connection with the Masons proved critical in helping him shape the Grange.[7]

Town life did not satisfy Kelley. After reading a number of books on agriculture, he bought land in Itasca—at the headwaters of the

Mississippi River—in hopes that the territorial capital would move there and Kelley could benefit from a ready market for his crops. Unfortunately for him, a split vote in the legislature kept the capital in St. Paul. Kelley then established the first Minnesota agricultural society in 1852. His personal farm operation collapsed shortly thereafter, in part because Kelley tied up his cash in a real estate venture called "Northwood" that went bust in the Panic of 1857. Portentously, volatility in railroad stock prices contributed to this financial crisis.[8]

After drought destroyed much of the rest of his holdings, Kelley moved to Washington in 1864 to serve as a correspondent for the *St. Paul Pioneer Press* as well as a clerk in the Department of Agriculture. There, he struck up friendships with men who later joined him to organize the Grange. These included William Saunders, who headed the division of gardens in the Bureau of Agriculture and designed the military cemetery at Gettysburg; William Ireland, a clerk in the Post Office and a fellow Mason; and John Trimble, a Treasury Department clerk and an Episcopalian clergyman. In December 1867, Kelley and his colleagues formally elected the first officers of the Grange in Washington, DC.[9]

Organizational Growth, Methods, and Structure: The Heady Beginning

Membership in the Grange was never larger than shortly after its birth in late 1867, although it came close to its original size again in about 1950 (fig 1.3). Grange membership swelled considerably before the financial panic of 1873 began.[10] But the panic made the Grange even more relevant: transportation-cost worries and financial irregularities (particularly among railroad enterprises) that surfaced as the panic spread encouraged the new farmer association to focus on collaborative enterprises and rate regulation. A number of financial institutions—including Jay Cooke & Company, which had helped the federal government with innovative financing techniques during the Civil War—failed during the panic due to railroad loans gone bad. This added steam to the budding farmer movement.

The founders of the Grange set up a temporary national organization, but they intended its structure to grow from the ground up, with the fundamental building block being a subordinate Grange made up of at least thirteen initial members.[11] Each subordinate was

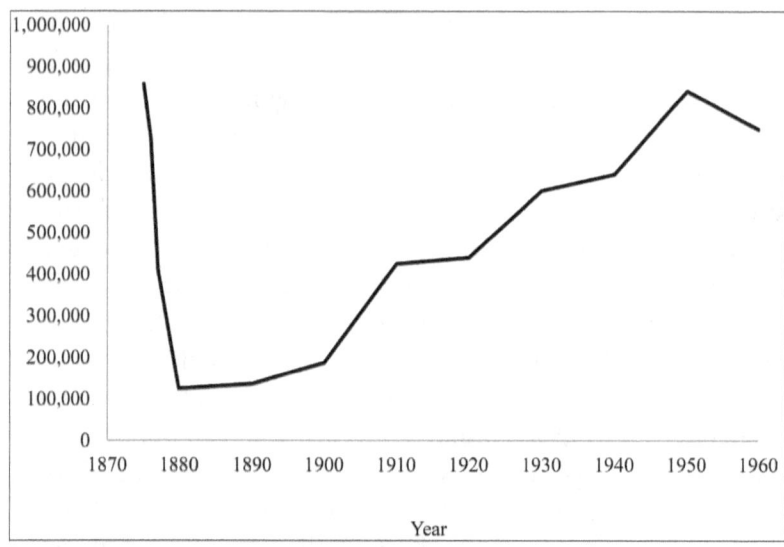

Figure 1.3. Grange Membership, 1875–1960. *Source:* Tontz (1964, table 1)

to have at its helm a "Worthy Master," along with other officers. Kelley and his companions envisioned an eventual web of subordinates spun across the nation, woven together to form larger county- and statewide Granges.

The beginning was rocky, as Kelley's initial attempts to inaugurate subordinates on his own mostly failed. Kelley organized the first permanent subordinate in Fredonia, NY, in April 1868 but was unsuccessful in establishing others as he traveled from Washington back to his Minnesota home. By 1871, four years after the inception of the National Grange, only 180 subordinate Granges existed across the country, with three-quarters seated in Iowa and Minnesota. These were arranged concentrically by date of creation around Oliver Kelley's farm (fig. 1.4). Only three State Granges had formed by 1871, with Minnesota leading the way in 1869, followed soon by Iowa and Wisconsin.[12]

Kelley then hit upon a surefire formula: send a paid recruiter to obtain an introduction to a leading farmer, win over the farmer by stressing the practical benefits of the Grange, and enlist the farmer's help in signing up his neighbors. Colonel D. A. Robertson, a fruit grower, journalist, legislator, and sheriff, spearheaded much of the early recruitment effort. By choosing respected men in the

Figure 1.1. Oliver Kelley Farm, 2013. *Source:* Photograph by Austin Wahl

community to lead the charge, particularly in the South, Kelley's army of recruiters soon met with considerable success. A. J. Rose, a rancher, farmer, and education reformer, was a prime example in Texas. Rose reassured wary farmers that the organization was fundamentally conservative in nature and pointed to its refusal to ally itself with the Knights of Labor (one of the largest and most influential labor unions of the 1870s and '80s) as proof.[13]

In Minnesota, many people organized a single subordinate Grange, but a few organized huge numbers of them. Among all those involved, 65 individuals organized only one subordinate each and 49 organized between two and four subordinates. An early success was T. A. Thompson, a State Worthy Master and a Worthy Lecturer for the National Grange, who organized 37 subordinates in the period 1870–73. Even more prolific was State Worthy Master George I. Parsons, a Winona farmer and lawyer who organized 87 subordinates, all in 1873. After his initial failures, Oliver Kelley rallied during the early '70s to organize 20 Minnesota subordinates single-handedly and cofound another.[14]

Recruiters changed the face of the Grange dramatically in the early 1870s. At one point, the rate of increase in new subordinates nationally was 2,000 per month. By 1874, the number of subordinates had climbed to 21,687, and only Rhode Island had no State Grange. Total Grange membership was 858,050 by 1875, with nearly half of all members residing in the Midwest. Iowa led the pack with 1,994 subordinates. Indiana had two Granges for each of the 984 townships in the state. Missouri had 80,000 members, encompassing more than 25 percent of farm families; and Kansas Grangers included at least three-quarters of all those eligible for membership. Out of a total of 834 subordinates ever formed in Minnesota, an astonishing 304 opened their doors in 1873, with 126 joining them the following year. The Grange spread into Canada as well.[15]

Small chapters proliferated initially whereas later chapters boasted much larger enrollment, although the pace of formation slowed. The average number of original members in Minnesota subordinate Granges chartered between 1868 and 1962 is 34; two enormous Granges sprang up in Mower County in 1912 with initial subscriptions of 123 and 133.[16]

A hierarchy formed above the subordinates. Once six subordinates had been established in a state, they could create a State Grange. After a number of State Granges emerged in the 1870s, a permanent National Grange solidified.[17]

For both practical and symbolic reasons, many subordinates constructed their own halls. Grange halls provided a centralized meeting place and displayed commitment to the community; they still dot the American countryside. Figures 1.5 and 1.6 show the Minnehaha Grange hall in 1945 and today. Grange halls often feature a raised platform at one end of the main room, various stations for officers, pillars and panels depicting Roman and Greek figures, and portraits of patriots and philosophers.[18] Chapter 4 offers more details about these grassroots operations.

The Role of Women

From the beginning, the Grange recognized the importance of family members working together to support the farm. To obtain a charter, a subordinate Grange had to consist of at least one-third men and one-third women. This mixed-gender requirement made the Grange quite different from nearly every other social, economic, cultural, and political association of the time.[19]

Minnehaha Grange Hall, 1945. *Source:* Minnesota Historical Society

Minnehaha Grange Hall, 2013. *Source:* Photograph by author

The emphasis on female participation stemmed in part from Kelley's devotion to his niece, Caroline Hall, who encouraged the involvement of women in the nascent society. Tellingly, Miss Hall suggested that females would add stability to the Grange because they would undertake all the routine work.[20] The Minnehaha Grange's experience offers some support for her view—although men served as secretary for the first ten years, women took over that role for the next seventy-seven. But women held loftier positions as well. In Minnesota, for instance, Sarah Baird organized three subordinates around the turn of the twentieth century. Mrs. Baird was a member of the Minnehaha Grange; she became the first female to occupy the position of State Worthy Master when she ascended to that post in 1894. Besides Sarah Baird, Minnesota boasted two other females at the head of the State Grange: Annie Bull in 1897 and Hildur Archer in 1963.[21]

Aaron Grosh, first chaplain for the Grange, took another view of female involvement: he thought women would elevate the tone of the meetings. Echoing Ole Rolvaag, author of the classic pioneer saga *Giants in the Earth,* he also worried about farmer wives ending up in the lunatic asylum if they didn't get out of the house more often.[22]

Although Grange tracts suggest that men and women were equal members, this wasn't quite true. The Declaration of Purposes is guarded: "We proclaim it among our purposes to inculcate a proper appreciation of the abilities and sphere of women." Grange discussions about economic policy and action mostly took place at county-level meetings of male delegates. For early Grangers, the women's chief role was to promote virtue in men and children. But if females played a somewhat lesser part in the Patrons than males, they also paid less: original initiation fees were $3 for men but only 50 cents for women. The Minnehaha Grange initially established monthly dues for men at 20 cents and for women at 10 cents.[23]

Masonic Overtones

Kelley's Masonic background had given him entrée into southern households as well as suggested a structure for the new farmers' organization. The Minnehaha Grange minutes from 30 September 1933 refer to the well-known anecdote of Kelley's meeting a young southerner who had sworn never to allow a northerner to cross his doorstep after Yankees killed his Confederate father, but who admitted Kelley because he was a "brother Mason." A case study of Black's Bend Grange in Alabama states that nearly every page of the minute book bears the "imprint of Masonry."[24]

Like the Masons, the Grangers wore special regalia, established a hierarchical series of degrees, and conducted a portion of their meetings in secret rituals. The Fuller Regalia and Costume Company in Worcester, Massachusetts, supplied jewels, sashes, and badges to the Minnehaha Grange and other subordinates around the country. The Fuller Company also sold Masonic jewels and apparel, as well as badges, flags, banners, and sashes to Civil War veterans.[25] Figure 1.7 depicts an early Patrons of Husbandry Badge, and Figure 1.8 shows the Minnehaha officers for the 1944–45 session dressed in their finery.

Figure 1.7. (*left*) Grange Badge, 1867. *Source:* Minnesota Historical Society

Figure 1.8. (*below*) Officers of the Minnehaha Grange, 1944–45. *Source:* Minnesota Historical Society

"*Our Agricultural Brotherhood*"

The ceremonial objects did not come cheap: in 1928, for example, a set of symbolic tools cost $3.75 (about $51 in today's prices), pins were $1.25 ($17 today), and sashes ranged from the "economically priced" $16.50 version ($224 today) to the model with fringe, tassels, and stars at $100 ($1,357 today). Regalia jewels in 1947 ranged in price from $6 to $15 ($62 to $156 today).[26]

Kelley viewed degree work partly as a way of educating farmers. Each degree requires candidates to listen to lectures about morality and focuses their attention on tools and symbols to remind them of lessons learned. For example, the first degree for males is "Laborer": it teaches the virtues of hard work and extols the nobility of agriculture. Symbolic tools include the ax, plow, harrow, and spade. Degree names are separate for men and women: Laborer (Maid), Cultivator (Shepherdess), Harvester (Gleaner), Husbandman (Matron),

Figure 1.9. **Degree Tableaux, 1947.** *Source:* Minnesota Historical Society

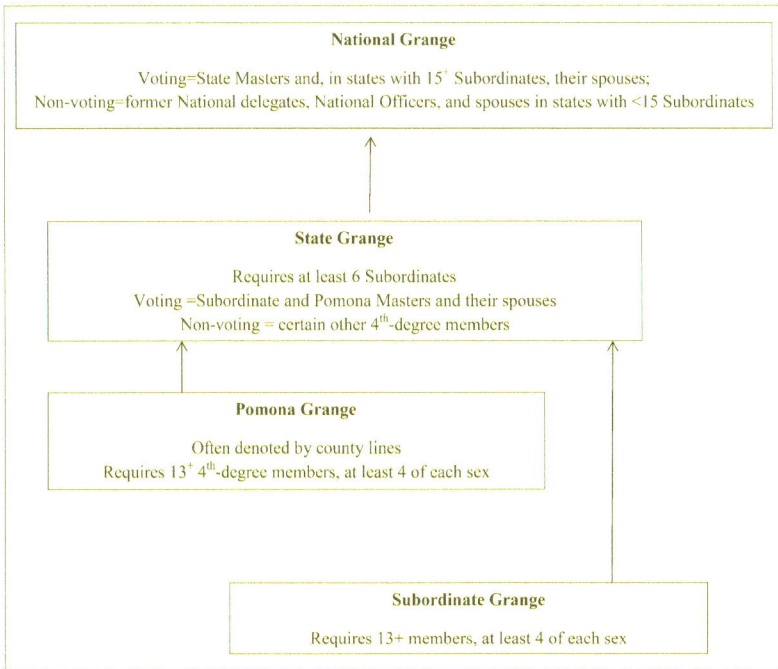

Figure 1.10. Organizational Structure of the Grange. *Source:* National Grange

Pomona (Hope), Flora (Charity), and Demeter/Ceres (Faith). These degrees create a hierarchical structure like that of the Masons or the military—fitting, as many of the early Grangers were also Civil War veterans. A degree culminates with a tableau formed by its recipients (fig. 1.9). Those who reach the fourth-degree threshold are eligible to form Pomonas, which are typically county-based associations.[27] Figure 1.10 summarizes the Grange organizational structure.

The preamble to the Granger constitution, written in 1874, uses (literally) flowery language to justify ritual. "Unity of action [cannot] be acquired without discipline, and discipline [cannot] be enforced without significant organization; hence we have ceremony of initiation which binds us in mutual fraternity as with a band of iron; but . . . its application is a gentle as that of the silken thread that binds a wreath of flowers."[28]

Although some people found the Grange's secrecy distasteful and refused to join or support the Grangers for that reason, others saw it as a necessary means of working out plans without alerting perceived adversaries. Who these adversaries were was not always clear, but presumably they included railroad executives, grain and cotton brokers, and warehousemen. An opinion piece appearing on 26 April 1873 in the *New York Pomeroy's Democrat* acknowledged that some worthy persons might not join the Grange because of the secrecy requirement, but "the end fully justifies the means. The evils and oppressions under which the farmers suffer are of such an infamous and grievous nature, that almost any means directed to relief would be justified."

The Minnehaha Grange minutes are rife with references to degree work and ceremonial rites. Meetings that welcomed initiates would "lower to the first degree," bring in the new members, then "raise to the second degree." Members routinely referred to one another as "Brother" and "Sister," and they (like other Grangers) referred to their leader as "Worthy Master." Each year, the National Grange supplied a new password to State Granges via cipher if all dues were paid. In 1924, amusingly, the Minnesota State Grange could not obtain the password because of noncompliance, but the Minnehaha subordinate—which had its affairs in good order—simply wrote to the National Grange to get it. At times, the Minnehaha Grangers chided each other about respecting rituals, such as standing up when the Worthy Master entered the room and using appropriate methods of presenting and retiring the flag.[29]

Granger Concerns: Economic Status, Self-Improvement, Political Presence

After the explosive growth of the organization in the early 1870s, delegates to the annual meeting of the National Grange on 11 February 1874 decided they needed to draft a more formal mission statement. The result was the Declaration of Purposes, whose ringing words open each chapter of this book. The goals are noble; the suggested means of achieving them are vague.

Bettering farmers' economic status held pride of place in the declaration. Grangers were exhorted to work together cooperatively, dispense with greedy middlemen, ensure cheap transportation, and break monopolistic practices. Oliver Kelley colorfully explained why economic concerns prevailed: "You must get into the farmers' pockets to reach their hearts, and a lively palpitation there invigorates their minds."[30]

The declaration emphasized more esoteric goals as well, including development of high moral standards and a devotion to continuing education (particularly agricultural education). It emphasized teamwork and fairness: "We appeal to all good citizens for their cordial cooperation to assist in our efforts toward reform, that we may eventually remove from our midst the last vestige of tyranny and corruption. We hail the general desire for fraternal harmony, equitable compromise, and earnest cooperation, as an omen of our future success."

The identity of the Grange came out clearly in the declaration: it was to be an organization composed solely of farmers—although some admitted members had only a tangential relationship to agriculture. What is more, Granger meetings were to steer clear of politics and religion—although not all Grangers stayed aloof from political matters, and most Grangers were solidly middle-of-the-road Protestants. Grangers were encouraged as American citizens to "take a proper interest" in the nation's politics and to have a duty to "put down bribery, corruption, and trickery," but were never to engage in partisan activity.

Economic Status

Calculating farm profit seems straightforward: multiply price by quantity to find total revenue, then subtract out various production expenses. Some (albeit scanty) historical data exist on the prices of agricultural products, railroad rates, farm population, aggregate farm output, and the like, but determining what happened to individual farmers' profits in the immediate postbellum period is no easy task. What matters to people, moreover, is not just net income but also the cost of consumption items, uncertainty about the future, ability to borrow in times of need, and perceptions of where they stand relative to others.

Several factors contributed to farmer dissatisfaction at the time of the initial enormous success of the Granger organization. These factors include farm prices falling faster than other prices, perceived exorbitant charges by middlemen and railroads, patent laws that seemed to favor the makers and sellers of farm equipment, heavy taxes on land, and regular upheavals in credit markets. At the annual gathering of the American Economic Association in 1893, Professor Edward Ross of Stanford put it like this: "A great cause of the farmers' [*sic*] difficulty is that he is selling at competitive prices and buying a great many things, including transportation, at monopoly prices." At the same convention, not-so-sympathetic Professor Franklin Giddings of Columbia thought the problem lay with the farmer himself, asking pointedly, "Why, throughout [the farmer's] long years of his affliction, has he always come off worse in the contest? There must be something wrong in his own make-up. . . . He controls more votes than other men control. . . . The failing is in himself. If you want to reach the root of the farmers' difficulties, you will have to begin with the farmers' minds."[31]

The latter view ignores something crucial, however: collective action is much easier to undertake when the number of interested parties is small. Transaction costs can impede the ability to speak with one voice, particularly when the parties are scattered and isolated from each other.[32] This is precisely the problem the Grangers set out to solve. The following sections take a closer look at some of the farmers' grievances that led them to find collaborative economic behavior attractive.

PRICES, REVENUE, AND THE PERCEIVED PROBLEM OF MIDDLEMEN

Farm prices did indeed fall in the first half of the 1870s, and initially they fell faster than other prices, as figure 1.11 shows. Perhaps surprisingly, farm prices actually started rising just about the time the Grange was enrolling members at a furious rate, whereas other prices continued falling. The relative volatility of agricultural prices was substantial, however, making planning difficult for farmers, especially because of the time lag between planting and harvesting.

Still, the total value of farm output rose throughout the nineteenth century, even adjusting for price changes over time. A measure that may shed more light on farmers' position is the size of farm output relative to the size of total output in the economy. Because farm population declined over time as a proportion of total population, standardization is necessary to ascertain the relative position of farmers. Figure 1.12 shows this: one line indicates the real output per capita economy-wide, whereas the other shows the same figure just for farmers.

Figure 1.12 indicates that, during the nineteenth century, both farm and overall productivity grew, but the growth rate for farm productivity

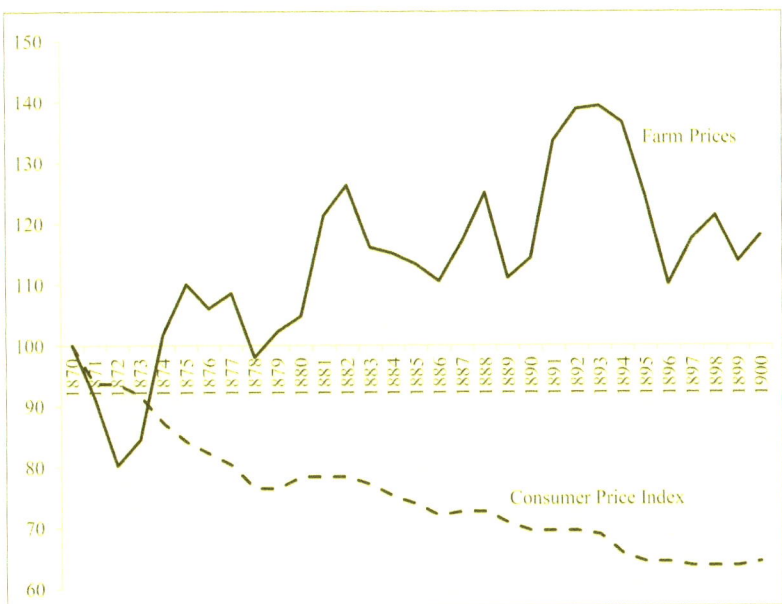

Figure 1.11. Midwestern Farm Prices and Consumer Price Index, 1870–1900. *Sources:* Bowman and Keehn (1974); Carter et al. (2006, Series Cc2)

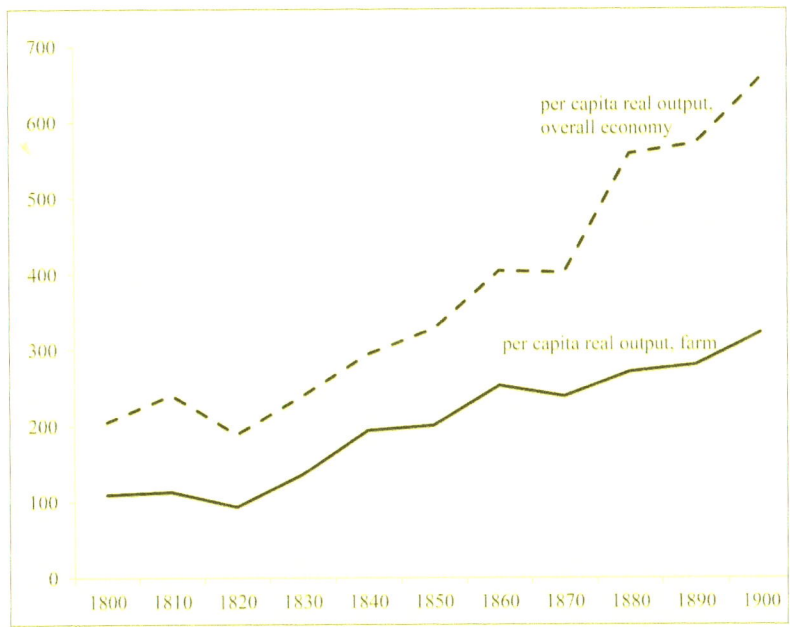

Figure 1.12. Farm and Economy-Wide Productivity, 1800–1900. *Sources:* Carter et al. (2006, Series Ba817, Ca11, Da28, Da1285)

stalled after the Civil War. The loss of so many able-bodied men in the war was a contributing factor. In the South, the end of slavery was also an element. Although plantation agriculture continued, the disappearance of the master-slave relationship meant less coercive power over workers, which was a factor that affected agricultural productivity. Black men continued to work hard, certainly, but many black women and children withdrew from the labor force.[33] The proportion of the population living on farms fell by 27 percent from 1860 to 1900, but the proportion of output attributable to farms dropped by 51 percent. These figures show that postbellum farmers were correct in thinking that as a whole they weren't enjoying the fruits of economic growth as much as others.

What is more, many Grangers thought that farmers did not get their fair share of profit because middlemen seemed to skim so much off the top. As the Declaration of Purposes put it, "Their surplus and their exactions diminish our profits." Brokers, warehousemen, grain elevator operators, and other sorts of businessmen who stood between the farmer and the ultimate consumer seemed to be parasites that produced nothing of real value but appeared to make a lot of money, at least according to Oliver Kelley. In his column in the *Sauk Rapids (MN) Frontiersman,* Kelley said that the agriculture problem was the antagonism between the producing farmers and the speculating middlemen. Kelley's followers agreed: the Minnehaha Grange on 19 May 1883 had a less-than-flattering discussion of middlemen, with Sister Yancy suggesting they all be "laid under the table." One of Kelley's dreams was to establish farmer cooperatives that would take the place of middlemen.[34] Chapter 3 discusses more fully how these establishments fared.

EXPENSES

Transportation Costs. For farmers the single largest change to the American landscape in the latter half of the 1800s was the railroad. Just over 21,000 new miles of track came into operation from 1851 to 1860, and a little more than 22,000 additional miles opened up between 1861 and 1870. But the next decade nearly matched the total of the previous two, with 40,340 miles of new track. Over 13,000 miles of new track came into use in the two-year period 1870–71 alone. Many of the miles added in the decade and a half after the Civil War were in the Midwest, particularly the Granger states of Illinois, Iowa, Wisconsin, and Minnesota.[35]

Farmers had complicated reactions to this enormous growth. Some had lost out personally in the Panic of 1857 (and thereafter) from worthless railroad stock or bankrupt roads that failed to pay off their bonds. Oliver Kelley fanned the flame by publishing newspaper articles about stock watering, in which companies diluted the value of existing stock by issuing new shares to the public. University of Minnesota Professor William Folwell suggested that Minnesota politician and Granger Ignatius Donnelly made farmers believe that watered stock robbed them by leading to high passenger and freight rates, whether it actually did or not. Many resented the sweet deals obtained by incipient roads: land grants from the federal and state government, tax exemption, and cash outlays from local governments to entice railroads to pass through their communities. Special rates for large shippers and free passes for public officials especially irked the smaller farmers.[36]

Yet farmers, like other Americans, recognized that transportation by rail for both people and products was often far more efficient than earlier forms of transport such as wagons. This was a double-edged sword: railroads potentially expanded the market that any one farmer could serve, but they also meant more rivals for each farmer. Farm values increased when railroads were built nearby, but this meant little to farmers who intended to stay on their land, especially because higher assessed farm value also meant higher property taxes.[37]

How a particular farmer felt—and how likely he was to embrace the Grange—depended in part on the presence of nearby railroads. No access to railroads typically meant more expensive modes of transporting goods and livestock to market, unless one lived close to a serviceable waterway. Consequently, farmers living in areas without railroads eagerly welcomed the possibility of the opening of a new line and were reluctant to engage in activities that would discourage railroad construction. Yet, once a road was built, its owners could charge monopoly prices until rivals entered the same market. With the entry of multiple railroads connecting one community to another, farmers more likely faced competitive rates and fares along that route.

The Grangers were particularly vocal about the "short-haul, long-haul" issue: farmers shipping their products to nearby locales often paid a much higher charge per mile than farmers whose goods traveled longer distances. In Minnesota, for instance, Rochester farmers paid 15 cents per mile to transport crops 45 miles to Winona, but Owatonna farmers paid only 10 cents per mile for a 92-mile trip.[38] (Note that these are the variable costs of transport and do not include the costs of loading and unloading, paperwork, and the like.) On 5 April 1884, members of the Minnehaha Grange asserted that farmers had proof of being cheated 30 cents per bushel on shipping and suggest that they would have to quit raising wheat unless an organized effort could change what they called an oppressive practice.

The difference in rates illustrates the classic economic power of a monopoly: the shorter the distance, the less likely a particular railroad had competitors for the route.[39] All else equal, a firm without rivals can charge more than firms that operate in competitive markets where consumers have more choices. This practice of charging two sets of rates fanned interest in finding ways to give collective voice to farmer frustration on the short-haul routes—fertile ground for the Grangers. As an editorial in the *Duluth (MN) Tribune* on 7 September 1883 provocatively phrased it, the railroads faced cut-throat rivalry and little profit on the through lines but then made it up with "extortionate charges for way shipments." The *Tribune* article applauded the "wholesome reform" suggested by the farm movement.

The Grange had a harder time gaining a foothold in areas with numerous well-established railroads. The *Philadelphia Evening Bulletin* suggested that New Englanders were less inclined to form Granges because they had less to complain about. In the first of two articles in July 1874, the newspaper rested its argument on somewhat shaky ground—it claimed that New England railroads were controlled by "moral suasion" and good government. The second article offers a somewhat more plausible explanation, noting the lower rates associated with railroads that faced substantial competition. Transport on the Chicago and Northwestern was 2.47 cents per ton mile against 1.50 cents on the Pennsylvania and the Erie and 1.57 cents on the New York Central. Passenger travel was 3.16 cents per mile in the West, but only 2.48 cents on the Pennsylvania, 2.2 cents on the Erie, and 2 cents on the New York Central. The article also suggested that the higher rates out west were especially annoying because western roads enjoyed heavy public subsidies.

State- and county-level studies indicate that areas with no railroad service were less likely to support railroad regulation. Southern communities generally seemed more interested in seeing railroads built than worrying about regulating them.[40] A letter to the editor in the *(Macon) Georgia Weekly Telegraph* dated 24 February 1874 warned that the "law of supply and demand" regulates prices but "when prices are regulated by artificial means . . . it is bound to work to the injury of some." It cautioned Georgia farmers that westerners' desire for cheap transport could in the end hurt southern cotton farmers.

California offers an intriguing contrast to other states because of different practices in storing and shipping grain: instead of using elevators, farmers placed crops in sacks in the field until ready to sell them. They then exported grain directly to Great Britain on boats out of San Francisco. Grangers in California thus directed their frustration, not at railroads or warehousemen, but at grain dealers who cornered the supply of sacks.[41] Of course, farmers could have avoided the problem by buying their sacks in advance. The lack of planning seems to have been due to ignorance of storage methods among new growers. One could consider the actions of the dealers simply as risk-taking, entrepreneurial activity rather than something more nefarious.

A look at the establishment of Granges by county in Minnesota in the period 1868–76 is revealing. Figure 1.13 shows that counties with railroads also had greater numbers of subordinate Granges. Some of this was undoubtedly due to denser county populations of agricultural families. The number of subordinates in a county is positively correlated with county population, with a correlation coefficient of 0.67.[42] Yet the striking success of the Grange where railroads had already been built is notable: people may have been reluctant to support organizations that spoke out against railroads when hoping they could attract one to their county, but didn't hesitate once the railroads were built. Grange activity—measured as number of subordinates per person in the county—was much stronger in counties with railroads, particularly those with only a single line.[43]

Borrowing Costs. Debt is a part of life for most farmers. The lag time between planting and harvesting means that farmers need cash and credit in predictable cycles, although climate and weather issues such

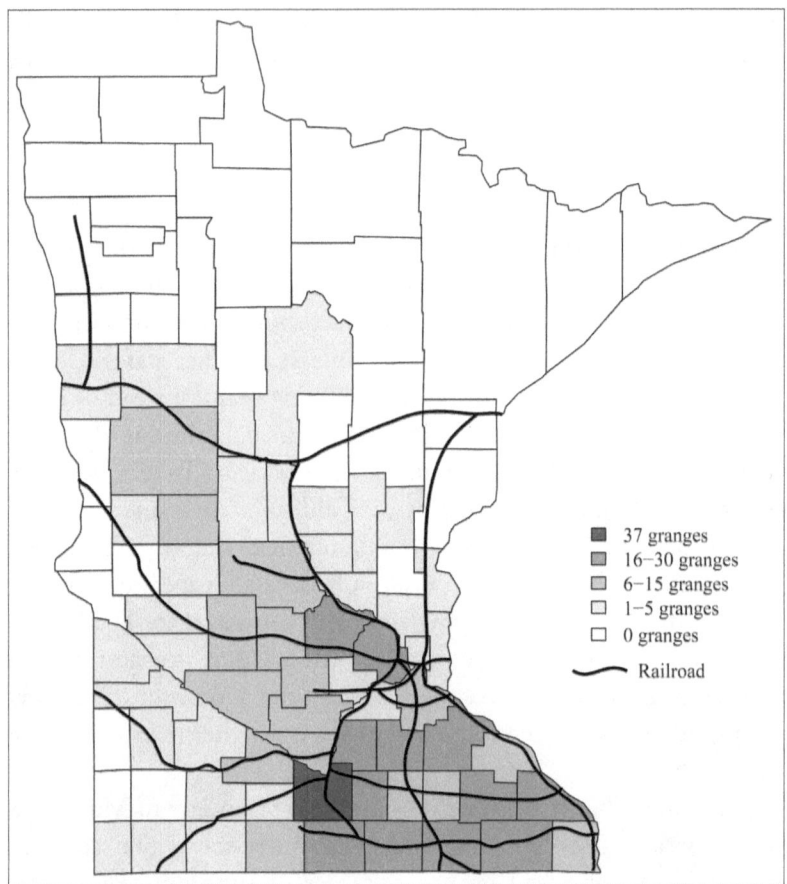

Figure 1.13. Density of Minnesota Granges by County and Minnesota Railroad Lines, 1874. *Sources:* Minnesota Historical Society, http://www.worldmapsonline.com/historicalmaps/kr-1874-minnesota.htm

as droughts, floods, and windstorms can undermine this predictability. In isolated areas, nineteenth-century farmers relied on local bankers, storekeepers, and farm-implement dealers for credit. These loans naturally carried risk for the lender: bad weather or pests could devastate the entire surrounding area. Risk led to high interest rates; in 1872, for instance, about half the real estate mortgages in the Dakota Territory carried rates of 24 percent.[44] Like transportation costs, borrowing costs were a constant worry for farmers.

The postbellum years were particularly difficult because many farmers had very little cushion. Discharged soldiers came home to find that years of neglect had taken their toll on farms. Abolition complicated matters in the South, as people had to adapt to a new sort of labor force. Because most battles had taken place on southern soil, destruction of property—including railroad lines and rolling stock—and disruption of land made things even worse. Families who had lost young men especially suffered. Low real wages for common soldiers during the war, coupled with high prices for many "store-bought" goods, meant that few farm families had any savings when peace came. Adding to these woes, the nation's return to a gold standard after the war led to deflation. To the extent that debtor farmers did not anticipate this, they had borrowed dollars at one value but had to pay back dollars that were worth substantially more.

Grange organizers stressed the potential of collective arrangements that could help ease credit problems for farmers. These problems became that much more acute just as the Grange movement took off. The Panic of 1873, sparked in part by risky behavior by some railroad companies, led to a severe recession and major financial upheaval. Foreigners were particularly reluctant to invest in US railroads, drying up capital even further.[45]

Taxes. Although the United States experimented with a federal income tax during the Civil War, this method of raising money quickly disappeared once the conflict ended, and it did not return until 1913 with the passage of the Sixteenth Amendment. State taxation on slave property, of course, also went by the wayside after war's end.

State and federal tax revenue came instead from property taxes (particularly on cultivated land), excise taxes (especially on alcohol), and import tariffs (mostly on manufactured goods). The Grange thus had little trouble persuading farmers that they disproportionately bore the burden of taxes in the United States, both on production inputs and on the consumption items they purchased. Oddly, under the Tariff Act of 1883 domestic vegetable (but not fruit) growers benefited from protectionist import duties, with the case of *Nix v. Hedden* confirming that tomatoes should be considered a vegetable.[46]

FARM VALUE: AN ALTERNATIVE LOOK AT ECONOMIC STATUS

The value of an asset reflects expected future flows—income and nonpecuniary benefits—yielded by that asset. Thus, another way to evaluate how well farmers were doing in the 1870s is to look at the value of what they owned.

Table 1.1 shows that, in real terms (using 1860 prices as a base), the average value of an acre of farm land was lower in 1870 than in 1860. Over the same period, average farm size fell from nearly 200 acres to just over 150 acres. Although the per capita value of GDP and per capita wealth fluctuated over the decade, the general trend was upward.[47] So, by comparison to the average American, the average farmer was not keeping up in terms of asset holdings. The Grange could and did exploit this discrepancy in its efforts to recruit members.

Table 1.1. Farm Number, Size, and Value, 1850–80

Year	Number of farms	Land in farms (000 acres)	Average farm size (acres)	Farm land & buildings Total value ($million)	Farm land & buildings Average ($/acre)	Average real value ($ of 1860) Per acre	Average real value ($ of 1860) Per farm
1850	1,449,073	293,561	203	3,272	11	12	2,431
1860	2,044,077	407,213	199	6,645	16	16	3,187
1870	2,659,985	407,735	153	7,444	18	12	1,839
1880	4,008,907	536,082	134	10,197	19	15	2,006

Source: http://www.ers.usda.gov/data-products/farm-income-and-wealth-statistics.aspx#27514, Carter et al. (2006, Series Cc2).

Self-Improvement, at Least for Some

Improving farmers' economic status was paramount for the early Grangers, particularly Oliver Kelley, and appealing to economic interests generated the Grange's initial success. But the inability of the Grange to live up to its economic goals also caused it to founder a few years later, as Chapter 3 discusses.

From the beginning, however, some Grange founders also emphasized its mission to provide for the moral and educational uplifting of the farmer.[48] Chapter 4 shows that these features of the Grange helped sustain it as a fraternal organization into the twentieth century and today.

Regrettably, the morals of the early Grange did not extend to welcoming African Americans into the fold, particularly in the South. Given that half of the people engaged in southern agriculture were black, this excluded a large swath of farmers. The first subordinate Grange in Louisiana—a state firmly under control of the Radical Republicans since before the end of the Civil War—reportedly let all join without regard to color, but this was not true elsewhere. A reporter at the *New Orleans Times-Picayune* asked National Master Dudley Adams in October 1873 whether a subordinate Grange would admit "colored" members, and he replied that this was a question best left to local interests. Some white southern Grangers organized blacks into a Council of Laborers, primarily in an attempt to groom blacks to be reliable farmhands rather than to offer them any sort of equal voice or treatment. The later Farmers' Alliance did not admit blacks, either. The Colored Farmers' National Alliance, the first massive black organization in the United States, finally emerged near the end of the 1880s.[49]

Race wasn't the only possible excluding factor. Article 12 of the Granger Constitution states that no religious tests for memberships would be applied. But the activities of the Minnehaha subordinate certainly exhibit a strong mainstream Protestant Christian influence. An entry from 6 April 1883 states that "A member of our order—when joining he confessed he was astonished to find so much of the teachings of the [N]ew [T]estament in our lessons—and when he was called south to organize a church where its members were composed of many denominations, advised them to organize a Grange instead, to avoid sectarianism and quarreling." Each meeting closed with a hymn, with favorites including "Blest Be the Tie that Binds," "Bringing in the Sheaves," "Church in the Wildwood," "Praise God from Whom all Blessings Flow," "All Hail the Power of Jesus' Name," and "Onward, Christian Soldiers." Members were exhorted each year (as least as late as 1962) to observe "Go to Church" Sunday in honor of Oliver Kelley's birthday. The chapter contributed funds to local Lutheran and Evangelical churches. These practices undoubtedly created a less-than-welcoming atmosphere for people who were not white Protestants.

Political Voice (But No Political Party)

The Declaration of Purposes emphasizes that the Grange is not a political or party organization, and Grangers could not talk about partisan politics, call political conventions, or nominate or discuss political candidates in their meetings. In the 1950s, for instance, the Minnehaha Grange refused to rent its hall for a political meeting, even though its treasury was in major need of funds. Nor would it allow the hall to be used as a polling place if doing so entailed the storage of voting machines.[50]

Refusing to align themselves with a political party did not mean that the Grangers failed to participate in the political process. Grange members in the Missouri legislature determined that they would "act as a unit on all questions of financial policy and political reforms, without regard to their former political associations, and that they [would] introduce bills providing for cheaper railroad rates."[51] Texas Grangers joined with Republicans at the 1875 Texas constitutional convention to defeat a poll tax, fearing that it would disenfranchise poor whites. And the first resolution by Washington Grangers in September 1889 was to object to the new state constitution because they considered public-servant salaries fixed at too high a rate. They also opposed its apparent welcoming of foreign purchasers of state land and industries.[52]

But the professed apolitical nature of the Grangers would come to haunt them. The 1870 census reports that 47 percent of the population identified themselves as farmers, yet only 7 percent of the members of the 43rd Congress (1873–75) were farmers.[53] One reason for the inability of the Grange to continue its initial success was the greater willingness of other farm organizations to align themselves with powerful political allies and to engage in party politics to obtain preferential treatment. Chapter 3 explores this more fully.

2

The Granger Railroad Laws

> We adopt it as our fixed purpose to "open out the channels in nature's great arteries, that the life-blood of commerce may flow freely...." We are not enemies to capital, but we oppose the tyranny of monopolies.
>
> —*Declaration of Purposes of the Patrons of Husbandry*

For some, familiarity with the Grange comes from awareness of postbellum laws concerning railroads. Yet the so-called "Granger legislation" and related court cases had little to do with direct Grange influence on the political and legal processes.[1] Still, if only by virtue of the nomenclature, a discussion of these laws belongs in any book about the Grange. Contemporaneous newspapers and commentators linked the Granger laws with the Grange. And the connection to the Patrons of Husbandry is strong, if not direct. The laws arose in states that had significant Grange membership. What is more, they dealt with transportation and grain storage issues and raised questions about the nature of public goods, both of which deeply concerned early Grangers.

The Granger cases are fascinating from a broader historical perspective as well, because they exhibit the first major invocation of the due process clause of the recently adopted Fourteenth Amendment. More typically associated with lawsuits involving civil rights, the Fourteenth Amendment formed the foundation of the argument made by corporations in the Granger cases.

The holdings in the Granger cases—issued mere months before the great railroad strike of 1877—mark a turning point in American law, because they held that the newly ratified Fourteenth Amendment did not interfere with the right of the states to regulate private enterprises that were "clothed with" a public interest. In essence, these cases blessed the new Granger statutes. Some view the outcome in these cases as preventing industrial enterprises from exploiting ordinary citizens, whereas others see it as a fundamental encroachment on private property rights.[2] Despite their significance in legal history, however, the Granger laws were short-lived and did little to affect railroad rates, returns, or construction patterns in the late nineteenth century.

Common Carriers: Are They a Public Good?

To economists, a pure public good is one that is nonexclusive and nonrival in consumption. In other words, no one is prevented from using the good, and my "consumption" of it does not affect your "consumption" of it. Few goods are purely public or purely private in nature but instead fall somewhere in between. A piece of cake is a private good (if I eat it, you can't); a streetlight is closer to being a public good (I can't prevent your benefiting from it, and my use of it does not fundamentally impair your use of it).[3] Complicating the concept of a "public" good is the fact that the public sector spends money on things that may not be pure public goods. Professional sports stadiums constitute one controversial example today. Many cities and states have chosen to use public funds or borrowing capability to finance these, although most economists consider them essentially private goods.[4]

Were nineteenth-century railroads public goods, and, if so, why did it matter? Almost all railroads were privately owned, but they certainly had some elements of public goods. Generally, anyone who could pay the fare or freight rate could use them, so they were non-exclusive in a sense. (In much of the post–Civil War South, however, segregation limited the access of blacks to rail transportation and forced them to ride in segregated and often substandard cars.) Provided that some seats or boxcars remain empty, my use of a train would not bar you from using it, so railroads were also nonrival in consumption. Certainly the public provided funds and tax breaks to railroads, and often gave railroads eminent-domain power to acquire land. The public also frequently awarded railroads a limited monopoly along a particular route. What is more, the Tenth Amendment to the US Constitution confers police power on states to enact measures to preserve and protect the safety, health, welfare, and morals of its citizens. The critical question was this: Were common carriers like railroads sufficiently "public" in affecting citizen welfare? If they were, the public had a right to regulate them, particularly when it came to the rates charged.

In the first giddy decades of railroad construction, a complication was that many states searched frantically for ways to entice companies to build within their borders. One inducement was to grant railroads a charter delegating to the company the right to fix its own rates.[5] Under Supreme Court Chief Justice John Marshall's interpretation of the contract clause of the US Constitution set forth in the *Trustees of Dartmouth College v. Woodward*,[6] states could not interfere with the terms of private charters after they were issued, even those extended to commercial enterprises. Some read the case as implying that a state could reserve rights to revise the charter or regulate the company, however. The public aspect of rail transportation plus the Tenth Amendment coupled with potential ambiguity in the *Dartmouth College* case was bound to lead to conflict.

The first blow to the railroads came two decades after *Dartmouth* in *The Proprietors of the Charles River Bridge v. The Proprietors of the Warren Bridge*.[7] Under an arrangement by the Massachusetts legislature, Harvard College, and various other investors, the Charles River Bridge Company enjoyed a monopoly for many years on its span across the river between Charlestown and Boston. In 1828, the Warren Bridge was built a few hundred feet away—under its charter, it could charge tolls until it had recovered the costs of construction and then would become free. When this happened a few years later, not surprisingly the Warren Bridge put the Charles River Bridge out of business. The owners of the Charles River Bridge brought suit, complaining that its original charter entitling it to set its rates essentially gave it a monopoly on bridge traffic, but a deadlocked Marshall court could not render a decision in 1831.

Justice Marshall died in 1835 and Chief Justice Roger B. Taney (who today is remembered mostly for his decision in the *Dred Scott* case) wrote the majority opinion when the court finally decided the case in 1837. Taney opted for a strict construction of the original charter granted to the proprietors of the Charles River Bridge, saying that a state could do anything not explicitly protected by the charter. In his decision, he said that the happiness and prosperity of the community should stand ahead of vested rights. This was seen by some lawyers and businessmen as a major departure from the Marshall court's interpretation of charters. Justice Joseph Story asserted this in his dissent in *Charles River Bridge*. Others saw it as consistent with ideas also found in the *Dartmouth College* case that rights based on a corporate charter had to be explicit, not implied. Regardless, the court's decision in the *Charles River Bridge* case set the stage for states to explore ways to draft charters with railroads that would preserve perceived state interests, including rate regulation.[8] Complicating the matter, however, was the fact that many railroads crossed state borders. This would eventually lead to federal involvement in railroad regulation.

Shortly before the Civil War, major rumblings arose against railroads. New York farmers protested what they perceived as discriminatory rates in 1858 and brought bills before the legislature for several subsequent years.[9] During the Civil War, opponents of the conflict and the Lincoln administration, known as Copperheads, also were strongly anti-railroad. At the 1862 Illinois constitutional convention, Copperheads successfully inserted a clause saying that all private property was "subservient to the public welfare." Opposition from railroads, led by Illinois Central president William Osborn and attorney John Douglas, helped defeat the Illinois constitution. The following year, the Illinois legislature introduced a resolution asking that railroad rates be restrained by law in the interests of general welfare.[10]

What Were the Granger Laws?

The actions in New York and Illinois foreshadowed what would happen shortly after the war ended. Between 1871 and 1874, four states passed legislation that regulated railroad rates: Illinois, Minnesota, Wisconsin, and Iowa. Wisconsin Chief Justice Edward Ryan, who wrote the key decision upholding railroad regulation in his state, had led the Wisconsin Copperheads during the Civil War. Support for similar legislation arose in other states in Middle America as well: for example, the Kansas Grangers passed a resolution in favor of Congressional control and regulation of railroads, according to the *Baltimore Sun*.[11] Although eastern states had regulatory commissions to oversee railroads, these bodies had no rate-making authority. The legislative action that took place in the Midwest marked a new era in the relations between private enterprise and governmental entities. Southern states followed later on. The Texas legislature, for example, in 1891 established the Texas Railroad Commission—the state's first regulatory agency—shortly after the gubernatorial election of James S. Hogg. (Hogg may be best known for the name he bestowed upon his daughter: Ima.)

In keeping with its activity during the Civil War, Illinois was the first state to establish a permanent regulatory agency to govern railroad rates. An 1869 Illinois law provided that railroads should be limited to "just, reasonable, and uniform rates" and receive "reasonable and uniform toll or compensation." But this law was neither specific nor effective. Consequently, when the state passed a new constitution in 1870, section 12 said that "railways . . . are hereby declared public highways" and ordered the legislature to pass laws establishing rate ceilings and prohibiting price discrimination by railroads. The new constitution also permitted legislation to regulate grain warehouses more stringently. In only 3 of 101 counties—all in the extreme southern part of the state—did a majority vote against the sections concerning railroad regulation. After the constitution was ratified, the Illinois legislature immediately passed statutes effectively outlawing any price discrimination by railroads.[12]

Despite having just two thousand miles of track in 1872, Oliver Kelley's home state of Minnesota was the only other jurisdiction to enact a stringent law as early as 1871. The novelty of trains in this part of the world led to a desire to document them: Figure 2.1 shows, for

Figure 2.1. First Locomotive into St. Peter, Minnesota, 1870. *Source:* Minnesota Historical Society

example, the first locomotive entering the town of St. Peter in 1870. The state established maximum freight rates and set up the office of railroad commissioner in the 1871 law. Although the Minnesota Supreme Court upheld the law, saying that rate-making power was implicit in the sovereign power of the state, enforcement was weak. Legislators in 1874 enacted a stronger law modeled on Illinois statutes and transferred to the commissioner the right to set rates.[13]

Iowa also passed a law in 1874 to fix maximum railroad rates and establish an advisory committee, but this body had little real power. A later act (in 1888) beefed up the authority of the regulatory commission.[14]

Like Minnesota and Iowa, Wisconsin passed legislation in 1874. Named the "Potter Law" after its legislative sponsor, the Wisconsin statute fixed passenger fares and freight rates as well as prohibited free passes for public officials. The practice of allowing public servants to ride free had long galled many citizens, who viewed it as bribery. One of the most enthusiastic backers of the Potter Law was a prominent Granger and the newly elected governor of the state, W. R. Taylor.[15] Despite Taylor's support, the Wisconsin law proved hard to enforce. On 5 May 1874, the *Hartford Daily Courant*—a nationally prominent newspaper based in an eastern city that was home to insurance companies and other businesses—suggested that the presidents of the Milwaukee and St. Paul and the Chicago and Northwestern lines would never abide by the Potter Law because they considered it unconstitutional. Confusingly, the article went on to point out what it considered a silver lining in this "peculiar war against the railroad"— the money of "thousands of poor people" had been invested in the western lines, and statutes like the Potter Law "will cut off even the smallest returns" and might prevent a renewal of the toxic "railroad fever" that had ruined so many pocketbooks. It did not acknowledge the inconsistency of assuming that railroads would not obey the law but that the statutes nonetheless would prove effective.

Although railroad companies may have considered the statutes unconstitutional, they wanted to have the law clearly on their side. They therefore brought a rash of lawsuits, the most famous being *Munn v. Illinois,* which actually concerned grain warehouses rather than railroads.[16] Their argument was twofold: maximum rate legislation effectively allowed the states to confiscate private property without due process of law and thus violated the Fourteenth Amendment, and state interference with a private contract was at odds with the holding in the *Dartmouth College* case.

The US Supreme Court didn't buy it. Although the majority acknowledged the importance of the Fourteenth Amendment, the court determined that, if the property in question was devoted to a use in which the public had an interest, it was subject to control by the public for the common good. In a momentous set of rulings, the court decided that any business that was public or "clothed with a public interest"—including railroads and warehouses—could be regulated under a state's police powers.[17] In the majority opinion, Chief Justice Morrison Waite reasoned that the great extent and importance of common carriers and warehouses, the large number of people affected by them, and the monopoly aspects of these sorts of businesses made them public enough to permit maximum rates. The court also ruled that regulation of a railroad was permissible unless the company's charter specifically exempted it. Building on *Charles River Bridge,* this unambiguously obliterated the *Dartmouth* precedent that had placed the burden on states to reserve the right to make changes.

Justices Stephen Field and William Strong dissented, saying that rate regulation unconstitutionally deprived railroads of their property rights. According to Field, this sort of restriction was not within the scope of state police power. It was Field, in fact, who forever associated the Grangers with a movement in the United States to permit stronger state regulation of private enterprise. In *Stone v. Wisconsin*, he stated, "I dissent from the judgments of the court in the several railroad cases arising in the States of Illinois, Wisconsin, Iowa, and Minnesota, commonly known as the 'Granger Cases.'"[18]

The Genesis of the Granger Laws

Despite Justice Field's indirect christening of the early midwestern statutes concerning railroads and grain elevators as "Granger" laws, several scholars maintain that these laws actually passed due to agitation by merchants and businessmen. In most cases, the Grangers jumped on board only late in the process.[19]

In Wisconsin, for instance, the move for legislation began with Milwaukee businessmen who resented the control over the grain business held by Alexander Mitchell and Angus Smith. Mitchell was president of the Milwaukee and St. Paul Railroad and owner of the Wisconsin Marine and Fire Insurance Company bank, which held 35 percent of the city's banking assets. Smith built the first grain elevator in Milwaukee. Through an exclusive leasing arrangement, these two men controlled virtually all the elevators in the area. Francis West, a legislator and Milwaukee grain commission merchant—but not a Granger—introduced a bill to reduce grain storage rates and regulate railroads. What ultimately passed (the Potter Law) was somewhat less radical than West's bill. Importantly, however, Grangers neither sponsored nor officially approved the Potter Law, although the Granger governor and the Granger Chief Justice of the Wisconsin Supreme Court expressed their support for it.[20]

Businessmen likewise were the moving force in Iowa. Preferential long-haul rates had deprived Iowa commercial centers of their former economic importance, so river-town merchants brought bills before the legislature in the 1860s asking for fixed maximum rates, improved water routes, and more control over the charters of new railroads. Grangers did not get involved until the 1872–73 session and were not primarily responsible for the statutes passed in 1874.[21]

Illinois and Minnesota had similar stories. The well-known "Granger Case," *Munn v. Illinois,* illustrates this. Messrs. Munn and Scott owned a grain warehouse, and Chicago businessmen worried that they were mixing together different qualities of grain. After a regulation required strict separation of grain grades, Munn constructed false bottoms in the grain bins to give the appearance of having more grain in storage than he actually possessed. The discovery of this galvanized Chicago merchants to shepherd through more stringent rules.[22]

In short, the Grangers were not chiefly responsible for spearheading what became known as the Granger laws. They did provide some support late in the process for the legislation, however, and they did promote an attitude of distrust and sometimes outright hostility toward railroads.

As part of their crusade against what they perceived as excessively high railroad rates, Grangers also were quite vocal in demanding improvements to other forms of transportation, including canals and rivers. At the Minnesota State Grange convention of 1869, members noted that railroad bridges caused congestion along the Mississippi River and said, "Its waters should forever be kept free and untrammeled and open to the use of every citizen within the entire navigable length."[23] Both the Minnesota and Missouri State Granges called for navigational improvements along the river.[24] William Windom, a native of Winona, Minnesota, chaired the Senate Select Committee on Transportation and submitted a report on 24 April 1874 calling for Congress to regulate some railroad operations and authorize an intense program of waterway improvement. As a consequence, the US Army Corps of Engineers went to work to establish a channel of 4.5 feet for the upper Mississippi via a complex system of wing dams and closing dams that are still in operation. The corps—the only formally trained group of engineers in the early days of the nation—was key in constructing and maintaining navigable rivers, canals, railroads, and roads throughout the country after the case of *Gibbons v. Ogden*[25] determined that federal authority covered interstate commerce. One of the more famous members of the corps was Robert E. Lee, who served in it for twenty-six years after graduating second in his West Point class of 1829.[26]

The Granger Railroad Laws

Backlash against the Granger Laws

The newspapers of the day had much to say about the so-called Granger laws—most of it unflattering—and fueled the public perception that the Grangers bore primary responsibility for these laws. Editorials speculated freely about the expected impact of the laws on railroad service, credit markets, and nonagricultural workers; they wrote acidly of the salaries of Grange officials; and they chided the Grangers for laziness, hypocrisy, and overreliance on the government. This was clearly an issue that created strong feelings.

The *Philadelphia Inquirer* from 15 July 1874, for instance, stated: "The Potter law is simply an act to confiscate property, besides a violation of contract between the bondholders and companies. . . . Slower trains and poor service is the legitimate sequence of this Granger law." In the same month, the *Hartford Daily Courant,* the *New Orleans Times,* and the *Baltimore Sun* agreed that the Granger laws swindled bondholders and would close the European market against new railroad securities. The *Sun* went on to say that it hoped commissioners were "satisfied with what roads they have" because no new ones would be built and the existing ones would go bankrupt because of the laws. Notably, most of these newspapers were published in large port cities, far away from Midwestern grain farmers.

Others besides bondholders suffered, according to the *(Macon) Georgia Weekly Telegraph* from 22 May 1874: "The war on the railroads by the farmers of the West has brought poverty to the home of many mechanics in the Middle States. . . . The Granger movement has thus indirectly deprived nearly a million persons of their means of support."

Grangers actually had it a lot better than other folk, according to commentators who relied more on bluster than logic or evidence. Although it gave no source for its figures, the *Hartford Daily Courant* on 13 April 1874 claimed that farmers made a 100 percent return in Missouri and a 200 percent return in Kansas, plus they enjoyed a doubling or tripling of their land value when a railroad was built. Yet these greedy people didn't want railroad stockholders to earn a return, according to the *Daily Courant.* The article did not explain why these supposedly enormous returns didn't generate an equally enormous population rush to Missouri and Kansas.[27] The

Philadelphia Inquirer snidely pointed out that the secretary of the National Grange earned $7,000 a year while the assistant secretary of the Treasury received only half as much. It went on to say: "This anti-monopoly scribe is also in receipt of numerous perquisites, and his office is financially worth more than that of the Chief Justice of the US Supreme Court, or the Secretary of State."[28] The article does not mention the huge salaries and company shares issued to contemporaneous captains of industry.

Accusations of sharp practices and malingering abounded. An opinion piece in the *Philadelphia Inquirer* from 30 October 1873 denounced the Grangers for doing exactly what they protested. It noted that the master of the Iowa State Grange issued an order prohibiting the establishment of any more subordinates within five miles of an existing one and concluded that this "so-called Western farmers' movement against nothing in particular and everything in general, is not that of a spontaneous uprising of agriculturists it professes to be, but a first-class monopoly."

In 1875, Charles Francis Adams Jr.—later the president of the Union Pacific Railroad—condemned the Grangers in strong terms in the *North American Review,* saying, "In plain language, they wish others to take all the risk, while they are to retain the entire excess of profit, which was the inducement for which that risk was incurred." Adams, a Harvard-educated lawyer who was the grandson of one American president and the great-grandson of another, fought with distinction at Antietam and Gettysburg and later led a regiment of black soldiers. After the war, he first ran the Massachusetts railroad commission but became frustrated by its lack of enforcement power and crossed over to the ranks of railroad executives.

The *San Francisco Evening Bulletin* on 2 June 1874 made a different sort of criticism. It suggested that, if midwestern Grangers wanted cheaper transport, why not build their own railroad, as had the Monterey County Grangers?

One commentator took the unusual step of infiltrating the Grange, then publishing the details of their secret ceremonies. His reasoning? He saw the Grangers as a thoroughly uncharitable monopoly out to "build up the rich and oppress the poor." This writer—clearly not an economist—was appalled to "see Patrons refusing to give the laborer employment, for no better excuse than that it is not profitable to . . . employ hands." He found Grangers to be un-Christian because they "complain of the grain merchants, but . . . in disposing of their hogs they seem to exhaust all the cunning, ingenuity, and espionage relative to a contract of sale." The frontispiece to his pamphlet described the Grange as "one of the Greatest Monopolies of the Age."[29]

Granger Laws Were Not Especially Effective in the Short Run

Contemporaneous observers perceived the Grangers as the driving force behind the Gilded-Age laws regulating railroads. Although this perception inflates the Granger influence in getting the laws passed, it is true that many Grangers—particularly the smaller farmers and those on short-haul routes—supported both the legislation and the court cases that upheld the right of states to regulate railroads.

Like many Granger efforts, however, these attempts to rein in transportation costs were not especially effective in the short run. The railroad companies successfully stalled some legislation and encumbered other statutes with exceptions. Wisconsin Railway Commissioner J. H. Osborn (a Granger) complained in the *Philadelphia Evening Bulletin* of 19 June 1874 that, whenever a railroad bill came up that was likely to pass, "the railroad men and their agents in the Legislature endeavor to load it down with radical amendments ostensibly in the interest of the public, but really seeking to make them so arbitrary they would be inoperative." The article went on to say that Californians had suffered the same fate when dealing with Leland Stanford's henchmen. After the Panic of 1873, railroad lobbyists convinced many legislators that their companies suffered such financial stress they could not afford to lower rates. And, not surprisingly, when legislatures chose to write laws that focused on outlawing discrimination, railroads responded by raising their lowest rates rather than reducing their highest rates.[30]

One newspaper report offered evidence that passenger rates out of Chicago did fall somewhat after the Granger laws passed. Fares into Iowa, Nebraska, Missouri, and Kansas fell between 1.8 and 12.2 percent, with most fare declines ranging from 2 to 6 percent. The article does not report the time period over which the decline took place.[31] Because prices generally were falling (between 2 and 5 percent annually) during the 1870s, these reduced rates are not clearly attributable to the legislation.

One test of the effectiveness of the statutes might be to examine whether railroads in Granger states earned less or built less track relative to railroads in other states. In fact, one study finds that railroads in the Granger states more than held their own in terms of earnings and construction. It concludes that the Granger laws had little to no effect on the profitability and value of railroads. A criticism of the study suggests that the comparison is flawed, however, because the comparison states with no Granger laws (Indiana, Michigan, Nebraska, and Missouri) nonetheless had active Granges that had similarly protested railroad rates.[32]

The Granger cases targeted grain elevators and warehouses as well as railroads. Although the effect of the laws on these enterprises is not well studied in the scholarly literature, one contemporaneous newspaper report suggested that warehouse storage rates went down as their owners anticipated the outcome of *Munn v. Illinois*.[33]

Granger Laws Were Short-Lived but Left a Long Legacy

Not only were the Granger laws relatively ineffectual, they didn't last very long. Shortly after the Supreme Court heard *Munn*, many states repealed the statutes that had set maximum rates and reduced the power of rate-making commissions. Even though the court had upheld a state's right to fix rates, the states and eventually the federal government moved toward a regulatory model that established administrative commissions whose rulings could be reviewed by courts. The first major federal legislation, in 1887, established the Interstate Commerce Commission (ICC); later on, the Hepburn Act (1906) prescribed uniform accounting and open books, and gave the ICC the power to name reasonable maximum rates.[34]

In part, these developments were due to the actions of the court itself in reversing two key holdings in the Granger cases. The first, that states could regulate interstate commerce where its citizens were affected, disappeared under the case of *Wabash, St. Louis, and Pacific Railroad v. Illinois,* and the Interstate Commerce Act of 1887.[35] The second, that state regulation of rates was not subject to judicial review, went by the wayside under the 1890 cases called the Minnesota

Rate Cases, headlined by *Chicago, Milwaukee, St. Paul Railway Company v. Minnesota*.[36] Regulation itself remained, although the nexus of control passed into federal hands.

The fleeting nature of the Granger laws isn't the whole story, then. As I discuss more fully in the final chapter, these laws raised important questions about the role of government in supervising and regulating private activities as well as the degree to which courts can oversee the actions of legislatures. These questions remain alive and well in the twenty-first century. Although the Granger laws themselves were short-lived, they nevertheless left a long-lasting imprint.

3

The Grange's Ambitious Experiments with Private Cooperation

> We must dispense with a surplus of middlemen . . . we do not need them.
>
> —*Declaration of Purposes of the Patrons of Husbandry*

Collective self-reliance constituted Oliver Kelley's vision of a successful Grange. Stung by his own business mishaps and frustrated by his interactions with eastern capitalists, Kelley wrote a letter to the other officers of the National Grange on 12 July 1868 calling for a network of Grange marketing cooperatives. He also promoted the notion of state agents purchasing supplies and implements for Granger farmers.[1]

The near obsession with middlemen even gave rise to a joke. In June 1874 the politically conservative, pro-business *Hartford Daily Courant* referred to the new game "Granger seven up," in which three persons play for a can of oysters. "The first man gets the oysters, the last one the can, and the 'middle man' don't [*sic*] get anything."

The collective efforts enjoyed some limited success, and some of them—particularly insurance and utility cooperatives—lasted into the twentieth century. Yet most early Grange endeavors failed because of inexperience, mismanagement, a lack of connection to political powers, or an inability to provide local farmers with what they needed most. An 1873 editorial in the *New Orleans Daily Picayune* cogently predicted why it expected failure: "We doubt the expediency of the establishment of factories to be managed and controlled by the Granges. Agriculture and manufactures are two wholly distinct pursuits. . . . The farmer will do better to confine his attention to that business which he understands."[2] This passage neatly calls forth the economic concepts of comparative advantage and specialization.

Attempts to unify production and sales operations initially seemed attractive, because they offered farmers the potential of earning monopoly profits. Yet standard game theory explains why such endeavors are so often unsuccessful.[3] People have incentives to agree to band together and restrict output so as to drive up prices, but then each individual has an equally strong incentive to defect from such agreements to grab more personal profit. Defection possibilities arguably were greater for some nineteenth-century agricultural products than for others—grain, for example, was easily stored and easily released from inventory, whereas milk was not.

Centralized purchasing was touted for its money-saving potential, yet many Grangers had misgivings about the motives of appointed (rather than elected) agents. They also viewed with suspicion the accumulation of funds in the bank account of the National Grange.

Ultimately, the Grangers discovered that middlemen were not necessarily worthless parasites and financiers were not always ruthless exploiters. Middlemen in fact had specialized knowledge and could perform useful services, and lenders who undertook risk could lose big—like those who backed Kelley's Northwood project—as well as win big. Businessmen and transportation executives likewise learned that farmers acting together were potentially a force to be reckoned with. Ultimately, however, the Grange found itself better able to support farmers in social and educational programs than in joint production, purchasing, and marketing efforts. Its cooperative experiments did, however, live on in more successful ventures undertaken by other farm organizations, particularly those focused on single commodities.

Early Efforts at Cooperation and Consolidation

The peak of the cooperative movement occurred in 1877, when about 30,000 co-ops existed. Various Grange mills, elevators, and warehouses flourished for a short while. Some cooperative buying of commodities and insurance saved members money, particularly at the Pomona (county) level, and cooperative selling, particularly via creameries and cheese factories, made a decent amount of money.[4]

Why did Kelley and other Grangers stress cooperation so heavily? In part, to keep up with everyone else. An address to the farmers of California in 1872 contrasted farmer experience with that of the typical businessman: "The very occupation of the farmers leads to an isolated life . . . to individual reliance. . . . On the contrary, the occupations of the manufacturer, the merchant, the banker, and the general business men of the towns and cities, lead to frequent intercourse and interchange of thought to associations and organizations, and consequently to collective, powerful, and successful effort."[5]

These thoughts echoed in an August 1875 editorial in the *New Orleans Times:* "The segregated character of the rural population of all countries has been such as to forbid the concentration and comparison of ideas so common among men in all other pursuits and occupations." It goes on to say: "One of the noblest results of the Granger movement will surely be the awakening of the best energies of farmers, by the frequent contact of mind with mind that must take place in meetings of the Order."

Minnesota politician and Granger Ignatius Donnelly (fig. 3.1) gave a speech offering the same solution: "[The Granges] can do for the farmers what cooperation has done for all other classes. The Granges will increase intelligence, and produce unity of action. They will cheapen purchases. Already they are able to obtain large discounts upon many articles. The Granges have become debating societies where the farmers discuss their interests."[6]

Figure 3.1. Ignatius Donnelly, 1880.
Source: Minnesota Historical Society

The Grange's Ambitious Experiments with Private Cooperation

Half a century after Donnelly's speech, Worthy Master Sarah Baird made an urgent plea to the Minnesota State Grange to remind its members of its mission: "The difficulty of organizing farmers in the west comes from the transient mixed population who live on a farm but a short period. . . . Lack of permanency and stability does not encourage . . . organization for economic social and intelligent improvement. It is up to farmers themselves to change these conditions." For them to be heard, it would take "cooperation . . . leadership among themselves, with an army of patriotic followers."[7]

One of the more ironic instances of collective discussion of Grangers' interests occurred in a Dakota Territory subordinate. Here, the members gathered together to agree on the wages they paid to hired hands.[8] Despite their indignation with railroads for monopolistic behavior, these farmers nevertheless saw the merit of collusive practices.

Cooperative Purchases

By the time of the Donnelly speech, the Minnesota State Grange had already appointed an agent, C. A. Prescott, to buy supplies and implements. Not everyone approved: Minnesota did not consult the national organization before doing this, and Kelley actually threatened secession when the National Grange dragged its feet in supporting the idea of a state agent. And some Minnesota Grangers resented having to pay a commission to the unelected Prescott.[9] Yet a March 1874 article in the New York weekly *Pomeroy's Democrat* claimed that the agent had saved Minnesota Grangers the considerable sum of $1.25 million on agricultural implements alone.

Other state agents reported initial success as well. Wisconsin agent Joseph Osborn issued confidential circulars in 1874 boasting of his ability to obtain garden seed from G. O. Hinckley of New York at a 25 percent discount, books from Marat of Philadelphia at 20 to 25 percent off, and parlor organs from the Prince Company in New York at 33⅓ percent off retail. Illinois purchasing agents reportedly bought a $100 wagon for $70, a $32 plow for $16, a $50 sewing machine for $30 and a $65 one for $39; they also saved $40 to $60 on parlor organs.[10]

Cooperative buying gave the farmers more bargaining power and helped them avoid retail markups as well as garner quantity discounts. Another advantage to bulk purchases was the assurance that farmers knew the source of the product. Clover grown in warm climates was not suited for cold territories, for example, and a single purchase by a state agent from a single seller helped reduce the cost of oversight on the provenance of seed.[11]

Many of the cooperative buying schemes organized around the Rochdale plan, a system originating in England that shared profits at the end of the year with co-op members. Rochdale co-ops maintained political and religious neutrality, which corresponded nicely to the Granger creed. Shareholders faced limits on the number of stocks they could hold and the returns they could earn, and each member had only one vote no matter how many shares he or she owned. Customers paid cash. Profit went back to the customer/shareholder based on his or her patronage of the co-op store.[12]

Cooperative Manufactures and Sales

Grangers engaged in cooperative manufactures and sales as well as cooperative purchasing. Mississippi Grangers organized two cooperative tanning yards, for instance.[13] *Pomeroy's Democrat* on 14 March 1874 applauded the flour mills set up by the Patrons.

Some Granges were especially entrepreneurial. The Iowa State Grange bought a patent on a harvester and built its own assembly plant. By 1874, Iowa Grangers also owned 53 grain elevators. Enthusiastic farmers even concocted plans to send both southern cotton and midwestern grain directly to Liverpool in exchange for manufactured British goods, cutting out brokers and middlemen.[14]

Examples from the Minnehaha Grange

The Minnehaha Grange reported several instances of cooperative efforts among its members. In November 1883, the Worthy Master urged members to save money by "unit[ing] in buying a winter supply of apples." As he put it, "This matter of cooperation has not been taken advantage of as it should by the Patrons. It could be a means of great pecuniary benefit." The following year, the group decided to buy sugar and cheese jointly. A cheese committee remained in place until at least World War I; committees to purchase farm implements and maple syrup also formed shortly after the turn of the century. Brother Baird announced in April 1902 his arrangement to buy ham and dried beef at a substantial discount. The subordinate began planning to purchase prunes from Washington in May 1911 and finalized plans in December. Minnehaha's Centennial History reports cooperative buying of staple foods and an elected agent who bought bulk quantities of maple syrup, tea, and vinegar, in addition to cheese, until the end of the Great War. During the war itself, the group accepted a proposition by some members to buy goods at wholesale and sell to fellow members if doing so generated sufficient savings.[15]

Cooperative selling and insurance also make appearances in the Minnehaha minutes. In 1879, an appointed committee of three began to plan a "concert of action in selling wheat." And, shortly after the chapter formed, it sent a different committee to "confer with some of the Officers of the Masonic Order in relation to the manner and form of Life Insurance practiced by said order and also to perfect a plan of life insurance and present [it] . . . at its next meeting."[16]

The Abrupt Drop-Off and Subsequent Regional Shift in Grange Membership

After the first flush of success, the Grangers nearly disappeared, particularly in the South. By 1877, the only former slave states represented at the national convention were Mississippi, Texas, and Missouri; by the end of the nineteenth century, virtually no active Granges operated in the South.[17]

Texas offers a stark case: the first subordinate appeared in Bell County on 5 July 1873. The state boasted 1,275 subordinates by mid-1876 with total membership exceeding 40,000. But, by the end of 1879, only 122 subordinates with 352 active members remained—on average fewer than 3 active members per subordinate. By 1893, a mere 23 subordinates existed. In 1905, the Texas State Grange—the last one in the old Southwest—disbanded. Arkansas has a similar tale: a single subordinate in 1872, a whopping 631 in 1875, but only 29 a year later, and none by 1890. Mississippi had a thousand subordinates in 1875, and none by 1891.[18] Texas apparently revitalized its State Grange in 1934, as it held its 79th annual meeting in July 2013, but Arkansas and Mississippi do not currently report any Grange activity.[19]

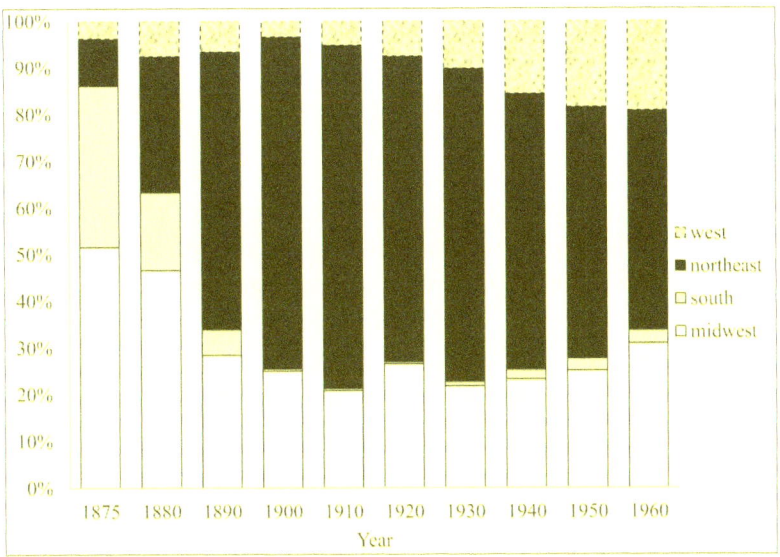

Figure 3.2. Regional Proportions of Grange Families, 1875–1960. *Source:* Tontz (1964, appendix table A)

The drop in membership occurred elsewhere as well, although the fall was not quite as dramatic as in the South. Chapter 4 documents the decline in the Minnehaha Grange in the last two decades of the nineteenth century. The *Idaho Daily Avalanche* (Silver City, ID) reported on 18 March 1876 that the Granger movement, which "swept like a tidal wave over the Northwest a couple of years ago," was rapidly falling apart, with 75 fewer lodges in Iowa as compared to the year before. Missouri had 26,000 members in 1873, 80,000 in 1875, and only 20,000 in 1878. The Dakota Territory had one subordinate in 1872, 56 at the end of 1874, but only 26 two years later. In 1882, the few remaining Dakota Territory subordinates annexed themselves to the Minnesota State Grange. Figure 3.2 shows the major regional shift in Grange membership over the first century of its existence.[20]

Why Did Cooperation Often Fail?

For collective action to succeed, people must perceive themselves better off than if they were to act alone. If realized net benefits fail to meet expectations, or if some folks agree to a cooperative scheme but then defect to serve their own interests, even the best-laid plans can go awry.

Regrettably for the Grangers, their early successes with collective action were not sustainable. Eventually, people simply stopped paying their dues, especially in the South. An exploration of the failure of an Alabama Grange reveals that members considered the programs dull as well as not worth the money. Apparently, the lack of economic benefit coupled with tedious meetings was enough to doom this subordinate. A financial panic in 1878–79 in the Southwest sounded the death knell for many Granges there when people decided the organization did little to help them economically.[21]

Purchasing Co-ops: Inadequate Inventories and Funding Fiascos

Most of the Granger purchasing cooperatives failed, particularly in the South. One scholar suggests that some southern farmers viewed the entire Rochdale scheme with suspicion because it came from a foreign country.[22] In part, the isolation and varied needs of individual farmers that generated eager participation in the early Grange also yielded its downfall. Cooperative stores did not always provide what farmers wanted in a convenient location, and scattered constituents made coordinating purchases difficult.[23]

What is more, many cooperatives operated with a minimum markup and no reserve.[24] When credit-hungry farmers found themselves unable to meet the Rochdale requirement of cash for purchases, these places folded due to lack of funds.

Production Co-ops: Ignorance, Mismanagement, Defection, and Corruption

Cooperative production efforts also largely failed. The Iowa harvester scheme quickly ran into problems when the State Grange couldn't fill orders fast enough due to lack of capital and limited management expertise. This Grange ended up bankrupting itself. Granges that established milling operations also found themselves wanting because milling technology toward the end of the nineteenth century increasingly became capital-intensive and farmers simply did not have enough capital.[25]

By the 1880s, most Grange elevators had ceased operation, in some measure owing to incompetent or inexperienced management.

Misguided Grange agents caused financial mayhem in both Indiana and California. Some people even blamed the Grange when Jay Cooke & Company went under in 1873, although Cooke himself attributed the bankruptcy to his inability to pay off claims after the Chicago fire of 1871.[26]

Sometimes the problem was an inability to get several people moving in the same direction. A description of the movement in Arkansas states that the Patrons accomplished very little because they would meet, pledge to do something, and then fail to follow through.[27]

When Grangers did succeed in putting together a cooperative agreement, the incentive to defect often proved too attractive to pass up. In both October 1873 and January 1878, a group at the Northwest Farmers convention proposed withholding hog products from the market so as to ratchet prices up. But many individual farmers could not manage financially and could not wait long enough to sell their goods at higher prices. The California Grange in 1873 tried to beat the middlemen—including their particular nemesis, speculator Isaac Friedlander—at their own game by withholding crops from market. But they also failed because they could not hold out forever. Ironically, Friedlander extended himself too far in 1877 and then went bankrupt, dying the following year.[28]

At times, the problem was ignorance about how a particular process worked. A scheme to sell cotton directly to Great Britain encountered heavy losses partly because the Patrons did not know how to select an effective Liverpool agent. When the Grange attempted to obtain favorable treatment from Cyrus McCormick, the developer of the mechanical reaper and founder of the company that later became International Harvester, he responded by saying he would be glad to dispense with the middleman provided that farmers could set up their own machines without expert help and would pay cash. McCormick quite reasonably noted that his field agents performed a large role in determining the creditworthiness of customers, collecting payment in a timely fashion, and assembling machinery. As one scholar put it, "The farmer learned that the despised middleman was an indispensable evil in business and that if he were to be eliminated he would have to be replaced by someone else."[29]

A newspaper editorial from the *Chicago Inter Ocean* of 4 August 1874 echoes Cyrus McCormick in dismissing farmers' requests for special treatment. "The idea is that government should make loans directly to the farmer at the rate of 3.65 per cent." If the farmer happened to have a surplus, "then the author of the plan says government should borrow of the farmer at the same rate, 3.65 percent. Here arises a query. Would the farmer do it knowing he could secure a higher rate . . . outside of Uncle Sam?"

Some enterprises suffered from ignorance, mismanagement, or greed, but others failed due to outright fraud. An agent from Waseca, Minnesota, embezzled $1,300 from the local Grange, for example. The National Grange caused several subordinates to be swindled when it endorsed an unscrupulous New York City firm. Oliver Kelley himself became embroiled in controversy. He helped his brother-in-law Robert Farley secure a goods contract; Farley then bilked the investors.[30]

These sorts of incidents caused many subordinate Granges to look askance at the National Grange when its bank balance exceeded $100,000 at the beginning of 1875. Pressure led the national organization to lend out these funds to the State Granges. When the State Granges had trouble repaying these "loans," they were renamed "donations." Most of these funds disappeared into failed business schemes.[31]

Cooperation and the Role of Politics

Although the Grange Declaration of Purposes clearly states the apolitical nature of the organization, the actual relationship between politics and the early Grangers was murky. Achieving cooperative goals but remaining outside politics was a tricky task. The Grange's perceived inability to navigate political issues in carrying out its cooperative endeavors contributed to its troubles and served as an example to later farm organizations.

Some doubted that Grangers truly could remain out of politics. The *Little Rock Daily Republican* on 15 April 1874 sniped that the Granges were "rapidly being converted into democratic caucuses or cabals. . . . Grangers' lodges are simply dens or nurseries formed thru the active exertions of the unscrupulous democratic politicians. . . . The granger movement in Arkansas has been entirely perverted from the original objects of the association into secret gatherings or clubs which are really controlled and manipulated by democratic politicians."

A case study of an Alabama subordinate and the minutes of the Minnehaha Grange suggest that these two groups adhered to the "no politics" stance, however, at least on paper.[32] The *Philadelphia Evening Bulletin* in July 1874 reported that Grangers worked with Republicans in Missouri and Democrats in Iowa. In the same month, *Pomeroy's Democrat* tells the cautionary tale of Good Hope Grange (Illinois No. 198), which dissolved itself when the Illinois State Grange nominated a "Granger" ticket rather than risk infighting at its meetings. This article warned Missouri subordinates that, because farmers made up only one-seventh of the population, they would have to work through one of the established political parties if they wanted success at achieving their goals. But sticking to the established parties wasn't always successful, either: Oregon Grangers nearly went bankrupt in efforts to influence politicians from the major parties, according to the *Morning Oregonian* (Portland, OR) of 21 December 1909.

Endorsement of Granger-minded candidates helped cause the near-demise of the movement in the mid-1870s, according to several editorials written a decade later. In 1886 the *Chicago Daily Inter Ocean* used this example of inappropriate political involvement to warn the labor movement to avoid making the same mistake. The *Duluth (MN) Tribune* of 21 March 1884 did the same to the farmers of the Northwest.

Yet others pin the decline in Grange influence to the rise of organizations like the Farmers' Alliance and the Greenback Party, which became politically active on behalf of agricultural interests. Ignatius Donnelly deserted the Patrons for the Anti-Monopoly and then the Greenback Party, which emerged at an Indianapolis convention in November 1874. Most of these political parties and associations were short-lived. Farmer organizations that officially began in the twentieth century, like the National Farmers' Union and the Farm Bureau, had greater staying power, as figures 3.3 and 3.4 reveal.[33]

Whether uncertainty about the Grange's relationship to politics muddled its mission enough to cause cooperative efforts to fail is unclear, but it certainly did not help them succeed in the nineteenth century. The next chapter offers examples of how the Grange

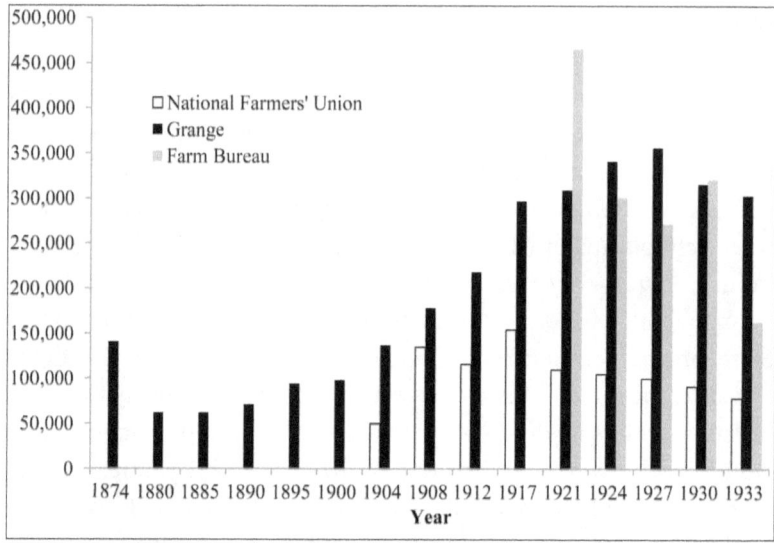

Figure 3.3. Farm Organization Membership, 1874–1933. *Sources:* Tontz (1964, table 1), Rothstein (1988, appendix)

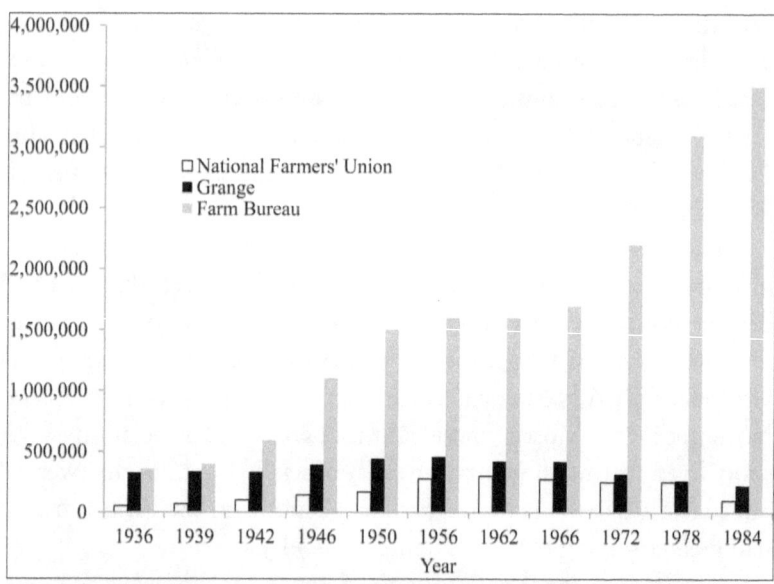

Figure 3.4. Farm Organization Membership, 1936–84. Sources: Tontz (1964, table 1), Rothstein (1988, appendix)

revamped itself as an organization with greater attention paid to social interaction, community service, and education. Part of its educational focus is targeted at keeping legislatures and the general public aware of the issues involved in farming.

Cooperation and Wariness about Secret Rituals

Secret rituals were an integral part of Grange meetings. Some Grangers suggested that these not only helped bind the members closer together but also kept outsiders from discovering or exploiting Granger plans, including ones to form cooperative enterprises. Oliver Kelley even created the degree of the Golden Sheaf, which he suggested could be so secret that the members themselves wouldn't know who the leaders were.[34]

But these practices bothered some potential members. Clergy for immigrant Germans and Scandinavians considered secret societies evil and portrayed the Grange as "the last hope of the devil." Scandinavians reportedly did not join the Grange in the Dakota Territory, although some immigrant Granges did spring up in Minnesota. Baptists in Owensville, Indiana, excommunicated Grangers from their church. When the Reformed Presbyterian Synod met in Philadelphia on 1 June 1874, a committee on the Grangers "emphatically and unequivocally condemn[ed] this and all other secret orders, as insuring deception and sinful in themselves, as prejudicial to the best interests of society, and as a lawless and inefficient way of obtaining a redress of grievances."[35]

The Methodists weren't quite so hostile, at least in Texas. In 1870, only 19 percent of Texans followed that faith, but 39 percent of Texan Grangers attended the Methodist Church.[36] Still, the secret aspects of the Grange may have meant that some farmers decided not to join, even with the promise of potential benefits stemming from cooperative action.

What Sorts of Cooperation Survived?

Despite the failure of many early Grange cooperatives, these experimental efforts provided a template for later agricultural groups. Two types of cooperative organizations have enjoyed greater endurance than the nineteenth-century Grangers: small, focused, single-commodity or single-industry groups, and the American Farm Bureau Federation, more familiarly known as the Farm Bureau. Some Granger experiments did survive, notably insurance and public-utility co-ops. But these enterprises are no longer run by Granges nor serve only Granger clients. Today's Grange devotes most of its cooperative effort to educational and social improvement in rural areas and community service projects rather than to large-scale economic enterprises.[37]

Single-Commodity and Single-Industry Groups

Cooperative efforts are more likely to succeed when the number of members is small and their interests closely aligned. Nineteenth-century Wisconsin provides a good case in point. By its nature, the Grange there included only farmers, but farmers were a motley crew—dairy farmers had different interests than wheat farmers, for example, and small farmers had concerns that often diverged from those of large-scale operators. The Wisconsin Dairymen's Association (still going strong in the mid-twentieth century, but now supplanted by the Wisconsin Milk Marketing Board, the Wisconsin Dairy Products Association, and other dairy groups) and the Wisconsin Agricultural Society, which operated at the same time as the early Grange, included owners of cheese factories and other businessmen as well as farmers. These organizations tended to have wealthier, more-educated members attuned to technological innovations in their narrow area of interest as compared to the relatively poor and less-informed Grangers. And it is these sorts of commodity- or industry-based groups that have had the most success in creating and sustaining cooperative ventures.[38]

Consider one of the best-known advertising campaigns of recent years: "Got Milk?" The California Milk Processor Board began the campaign in 1993 and later licensed it for use by milk processors and dairy farmers.[39] Another example is "Beef: It's What's for Dinner," with spokesman Matthew McConaughey, which is sponsored by the National Cattlemen's Beef Association (NCBA).

These cooperative ventures are not sustained completely by private associations, however. The NCBA is funded partly by membership dues and partly through the Beef Checkoff, which imposes a mandatory tax each time a head of cattle is sold. Congress authorized the tax via the Beef Promotion and Research Act of 1985, and the Supreme Court ruled it constitutional in *Johanns v. Livestock Marketing Association*.[40]

Piggybacking on the NCBA effort, the National Christmas Tree Association successfully inserted a mandatory 15-cent tax on Christmas trees into the 2013 Farm Bill. The tax revenue is intended to launch a "program of promotion, research, evaluation, and information designed to strengthen the Christmas tree industry's position in the marketplace; maintain and expand existing markets for Christmas trees; and to carry out programs, plans, and projects designed to provide maximum benefits to the Christmas tree industry" and to "enhance the image of Christmas trees and the Christmas tree industry in the United States."[41] These examples show that "private" cooperation may actually be aided by substantial governmental support—which could be part of the reason that Grange co-ops did not succeed.

Other Large Farmer Organizations

When the Grange shrank in importance in the 1880s and thereafter, more radical farm organizations sprang up which had lower dues and simpler rituals and sometimes offered credit to their members. Florida Grangers defected to more militant organizations as early as the end of the 1870s. As mentioned earlier, Minnesotan Ignatius Donnelly broke off his relationship with the Grange late in 1873 to help form new political parties such as the Greenback Party and People's Party. A Chicago-based group called the National Farmers' Alliance (also known as the Northern Farmers' Alliance) placed significant factions in the Iowa and Minnesota legislatures in the late 1880s. Two large agricultural organizations formed in Texas: the National Farmers' Alliance and Industrial Union (NFAIU, also known as the Southern Farmers' Alliance) in 1877 and the National Farmers' Union (NFU) in 1902. The successor organization to the NFAIU immediately leapt into political action when it supported a boycott of the jute trust in the late 1880s.[42]

Some radical movements began within the Grange itself. William Bouck, who took over the Washington State Grange in 1917, was the first State Worthy Master to be expelled from the national organization when he advocated fighting against capitalism, refusing to pay taxes, and declining to serve in the military unless the country was being invaded. Frustrated by an organization that he perceived as too focused on tame issues and fraternal rather than political activity, Bouck began the Western Progressive Farmers in 1921 and worked with the Communist Party to form the Progressive Farmers of America in 1926.[43]

These organizations, like the Grange, had problems getting co-ops off the ground and securing dues payment by members.[44] The only one mentioned above that still has a relatively large number of members is the NFU, representing an estimated quarter of a million farm families.

By far the most successful of the post-Grange agricultural organizations is the Farm Bureau. Some have characterized the Farm Bureau as a powerful farm organization but not clearly a small-farmer or farm-worker organization.[45] Farm worker and activist Cesar Chavez certainly found himself in opposition to Farm Bureau policy many times. For example, his 24-day fast in 1972 was to protest a Farm Bureau–supported Arizona law barring farm workers from boycotts and strikes and restricting collective bargaining.[46]

Agricultural historian Lowell Dyson claims that the Farm Bureau shows little sympathy to small farmers and farm workers and notes that the first bureau was housed within the local chamber of commerce. This contrasts with the Grange's relationship to business: when the National Grange realized that organizations in Boston and New York in the mid-1870s included mostly grain dealers and commission men, it revoked their charters. As late as 1910, Oregon State Master Austin Buxton warned against a "too active increase in membership of Grangers near larger cities," saying membership should be restricted to those engaged in agricultural pursuits.[47]

The Farm Bureau thus may more closely resemble the large farmers of the California State Agricultural Society, who viewed railroads as a part of the essential business of the state. The California Grangers, in contrast, were primarily small-scale farmers who joined laborers and small merchants to back legislation in 1876 that prohibited perceived discriminatory railroad practices. The two groups clashed on other grounds as well. The Grangers resented the enormous tracts of land granted to the railroads by the federal government and concentrated in a few hands; the society thought this concentration was a transitory issue as holders would eventually sell off the land as it increased in value. What is more, the small-farmer Grangers were suspicious of Chinese laborers and saw them as potential rivals, whereas the large farmers viewed the Chinese as a cheap and pliable labor force essential for their operations.[48]

Something that the Grange and the Farm Bureau have in common, however, is their emphasis on farmer education. The Farm Bureau has had notable success in this area, in part because it grew out of the extension education movement that originated in the land-grant colleges. The Morrill Act of 2 July 1862 established the land-grant schools, and the Hatch Act of 1887 initiated agricultural experimental stations.[49] The extension concept took root in the early 1900s, particularly when the infestation of the boll weevil gave rise to the idea of traveling educators, or county agents, who literally took to the fields to tackle agricultural issues in a hands-on fashion. Local Farm Bureaus form the organizational network to further the extension education efforts of the county agent.[50] Part of the Farm Bureau's success is likely due to its close association with large public universities and, thus, state budgets.

The Grange sometimes joins with other farm organizations—for instance, it formed a coalition with the NFU and the Farm Bureau to lobby President Herbert Hoover in 1932 for farm relief. The minutes of the Minnehaha Grange show a wary détente with the local Farm Bureau. The two occasionally held joint meetings.[51] Yet a report read at the State Grange meeting on 20 January 1923 urged local Granges to work with the Farm Bureau but to take care not to lose their own identity.

The Grange Regroups

After the first frenzied burst of activity, Grange membership through about the Second World War appears related to the stability (or lack thereof) in financial markets and the level and volatility of farm income. Following the Panic of 1873, two additional significant financial crises occurred within the next quarter-century—one in 1893 and the other in 1907. Financial markets remained unsettled until the creation of the Federal Reserve System in 1913. Figure 3.5 shows how Minnesota

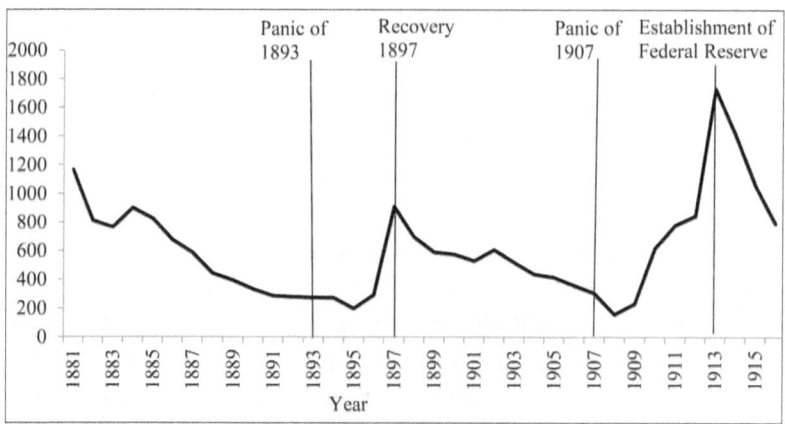

Figure 3.5. Membership Reported to Minnesota State Grange, 1881–1916. *Source:* Minnesota Historical Society

Grange membership fluctuated through this period, with upsurges occurring in the aftermath of financial turmoil and downswings once stability emerged. Michigan likewise had a rise in membership in the early twentieth century, when the state added 64 subordinates and 2,000 members for total of 28,000 members in 1900. By 1911, Michigan membership had risen to 60,000 members. The Pennsylvania Grange also enjoyed a large increase in membership that year.[52]

After the establishment of the Federal Reserve until about 1930, Grange membership often moved in the opposite direction from farm income. Figure 3.6 shows the percentage change in Grange membership plotted against the percentage change in per capita real farm income. For most years between 1918 and 1930, when per capita real farm income was increasing (the percent change was positive), Grange membership was falling (the percent change was negative) or remaining steady. But when per capita real farm income fell drastically in the immediate postwar period, Grange membership skyrocketed soon after.

The relationship between farm income and Grange membership weakened after 1930 when farmers had alternative agricultural associations they could join. Still, the dustbowl '30s saw renewed interest in establishing Grange subordinates. The next chapter records the escalation in membership in and attendance at the Minnehaha Grange during this time. In the baker's dozen of years from 1929 through 1941, 120 new chapters formed in Minnesota. In the two previous 13-year periods, only 45 (1916–28) and 49 (1903–15) subordinates began, whereas in the subsequent period only 46 (1942–54) subordinates

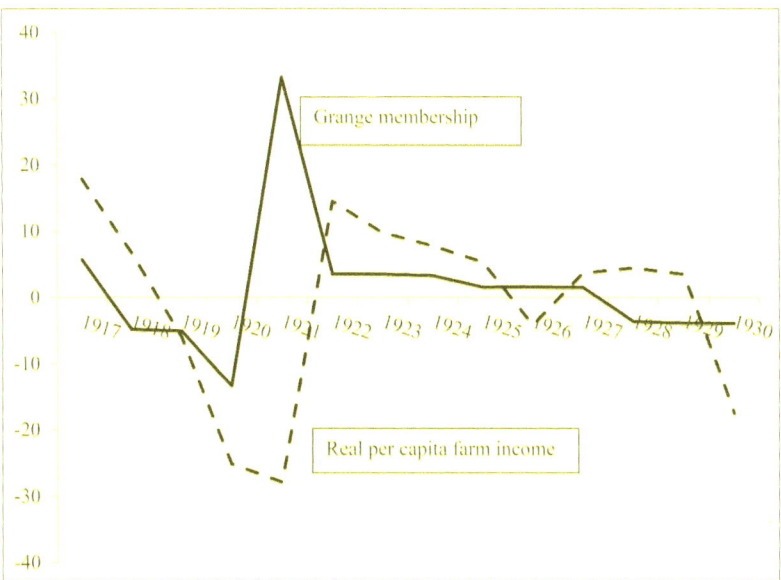

Figure 3.6. Percent Change in Grange Membership and Real Per Capita Farm Income, 1917–30. *Sources:* Rothstein (1988, appendix); Carter et al. (2006, Series Da1, Da14, Da28, Da1066); http://www.bls.gov.org/cpi/

were launched.[53] After the mid-1950s, when the farm population shrank substantially and farm size grew significantly, many subordinates began to close their doors or merge with nearby chapters.

Granges currently operate in thirty-six states and the District of Columbia. Although the official number of members is apparently confidential, the Linked-In profile for the National Grange states that it has "more than 160,000 members."[54]

Some Grange cooperative enterprises, particularly insurance and power cooperatives, survived through the twentieth century.[55] One of the oldest Grange insurance enterprises is the Grange Insurance Group, a mutual property-casualty company established in 1894 to serve Western Grangers. It now operates in Washington, Oregon, Idaho, Colorado, Wyoming, and California. Its members have expanded beyond Grangers, partly to diversify its risk pool and to acknowledge the decline in eligible farmers, but perhaps also to address a free-rider issue the Minnehaha Grangers noticed—that people joined the group merely to take advantage of the insurance offerings.[56] By permitting non-Grangers to purchase Grange insurance, the Patrons encouraged membership only for those truly interested in the Grange itself. The Grange Insurance Group's website nevertheless still stresses its "commitment to families in 'Main Street' towns, farm communities, and suburban areas of the West" and its "Steadfast Rural Values."[57]

Another example of a Grange-created insurance enterprise is Grange Insurance Services, Inc., which began providing automobile insurance to members of the Ohio State Grange in 1933. Re-formed as the Grange Mutual Casualty Company two years later, it started writing general property-casualty insurance, again only to Grange members. The company added hospitalization, general liability, and fire policies during the 1940s and 1950s. In 1958, the company split from the Ohio State Grange and began offering policies to the general public.[58]

Minutes from the Minnehaha Grange report frequent discussions of Granger-provided insurance. The entry for 6 January 1934 refers to a farmers' exchange providing auto insurance in Los Angeles, for instance. Members are exhorted to purchase Grange auto and fire insurance multiple times throughout the 1950s.[59]

Not only did twentieth-century Grangers promote insurance, they also took up the cause of rural electrification. The Grangers' fight to provide electricity at reasonable rates to rural areas in the 1920s and 1930s strongly resembles the struggle to tame railroads a half-century earlier. Again the controversy centered on the right of a private company to earn profits versus the right of the public to enjoy the benefits of quasi-public goods. Memorably named legislator Homer T. Bone solicited the support of the Washington State Grange to sponsor a bill permitting rural residents to form public utility districts. Bone and the Grange called for municipal corporations that would provide utility service without profit, operate under the supervision of a board of elected citizens, have authority to issue revenue bonds, and use eminent domain to take over the properties of a private power company if that company refused to sell. In 1930, 54 percent of Washington voters approved the measure. The neighboring Oregon State Grange successfully pushed through a similar law the same year.[60] Residents of these two states, plus those in California and Nebraska, continue to form public utility districts to provide water and sewage treatment as well as electricity under this sort of legislation.

Correspondence for the Minnehaha Grange reveals a letter dated 16 February 1927 from the Deputy Commissioner of the

Minnesota Department of Agriculture that sets forth the articles of incorporation and bylaws for a cooperative gas association.[61] (The chapter never actually set up a gas co-op.) More recently, the city of Minneapolis contemplated taking over the provision of electricity and gas in the wake of an enormous storm that left residents without electricity for days in June 2013. Enthusiasm for the takeover has since waned.[62]

The Grange helped launch insurance and nonprofit utility provision for its members, but these enterprises are now mostly under non-Grange oversight and serve a far broader constituency than just the Grangers. As the next chapter discusses, today's National and State Granges devote resources principally to legislative activity, whereas the main focus of most subordinate Granges is community service, social interaction, and leadership development among its members. The pattern of recruitment in twentieth-century Minnesota (fig. 3.7) shows

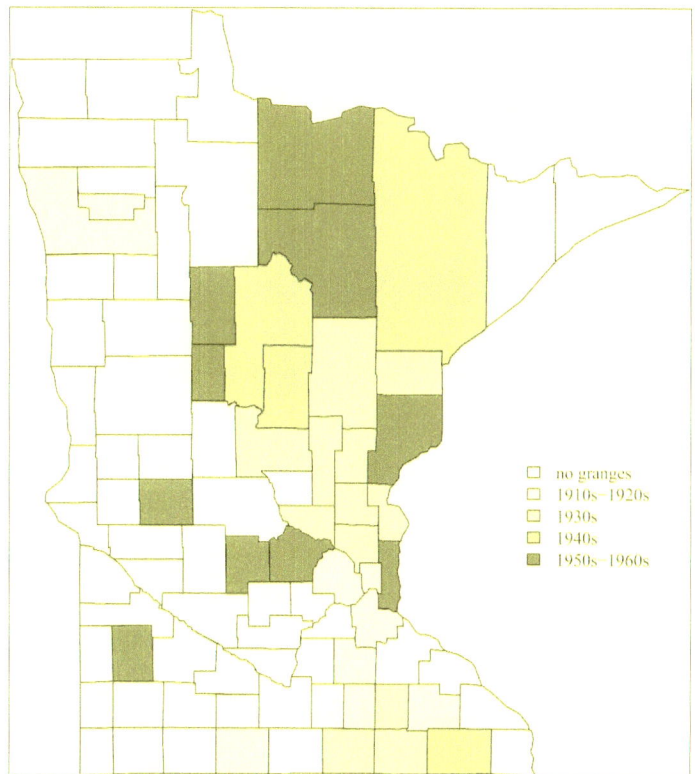

Figure 3.7. Establishment of Newly Organized Minnesota Granges by County, 1900–1970. *Source:* Minnesota Historical Society

that the Patrons have had their greatest recent success in out-state farming areas with low population density. The dates indicated show the decades in which new Granges came into being in each county. The map suggests that the social and fraternal aspects of the Grange are valuable attributes for its current members.

4

The Grange as a Fraternal, Educational, and Charitable Organization

The Minnehaha Grange as a Case Study

> We shall endeavor . . . to develop a better and higher manhood and womanhood among ourselves. . . . . We shall advance the cause of education. . . . It shall be an abiding principle to relieve any of our suffering brotherhood by any means at our command.
>
> —*Declaration of Purposes of the Patrons of Husbandry*

In 1879, National Worthy Master Jonathan Woodman became alarmed at the enormous erosion in membership, so he refocused the mission of the Grange to emphasize education, fraternity, and legislative action.[1] Although these features of the Grange existed from the beginning, they had taken a back seat to economic issues. When the Patrons' early attempts at economic cooperation and political participation proved less than successful, Woodman and others helped sustain the organization by promoting its social and educational aspects. As mentioned in the preceding chapter, this new emphasis attracted farmers in the

Northeast to the Grange—or at least deterred them from leaving in large numbers. The Grange also appointed a Washington lobbyist in 1919 and bought a building in Washington, DC, in 1943 to serve as permanent national headquarters.[2]

Woodman's vision reverberates in the words of Worthy Master Herschel Newsom at the 100th annual meeting of the National Grange, held in Minneapolis in 1966: "We must continue to emphasize the beauty and high privilege of rural life; its rich rewards, and its inspirational background which gives birth to a keener perception of mind and a sharper focus of action. We must continue to reason together for our mutual instruction and protection to lighten labor by diffusing a knowledge of our aims and purposes, by improving the communities in which we live and serve, by enriching our minds, and by constantly seeking to develop a higher manhood and womanhood among ourselves."

The records of one Minnesota subordinate furnish substantial information about how Granges operated, what issues occupied them, and how they carried out their mission. What follows is an in-depth look at how this Grange—the Minnehaha—financed itself, promoted education on a variety of topics, attempted to influence local and national legislation, participated in service projects, and enjoyed the benefits of community even as it sometimes suffered the consequences of shirking.

The Minnehaha Grange: A Thumbnail Sketch

Minnesota Grange No. 398 (the "Minnehaha") began operation in December 1873 in the village of Edina, now an affluent suburb of Minneapolis. The first members came from the Lyceum Society, a group of farmers who gathered periodically for literary and social pursuits. The association sprang up near a mill on Minnehaha Creek owned by George Millam, who was initially denied Grange membership because he was not a farmer. (He was later inducted.) The last official minutes were recorded in September 1978, although the chapter filed a community service report in 1985 listing 20 active members, mostly senior citizens. The Minnehaha Centennial History claims Oliver Kelley as the chapter's founder, but the State Grange reports W. S. Chowen as the official organizer of this

Figure 4.1. First Worthy Master James A. Bull, Minnehaha Grange. *Source:* Minnesota Historical Society

subordinate.³ The first Worthy Master of the Minnehaha was James A. Bull, pictured in figure 4.1.

Meetings of the Minnehaha occurred faithfully twice a month from September through May, usually on Saturdays.⁴ The first meeting each fall included a large and exuberant corn feed. On only two occasions—in January and February 1883—did weather keep the Minnehaha Patrons from gathering. Given that this was the beginning of the "Little Ice Age" when the January average temperature in Minneapolis was -3° F and the low hit -36° F, staying home seems quite reasonable.[5]

Members initially took turns hosting meetings. In January 1875, the Minnehaha began planning to build its own hall. The Patrons themselves donated most of the work, so the out-of-pocket cost was a modest $400 for materials (about $8,500 in today's dollars). The new hall (pictured in chapter 1) opened its doors in 1880. The first item on the agenda was a motion to buy several spittoons.

The eager attitude displayed in constructing the hall soon wore off. A waspish entry from 1883 states, "[I'm] sorry to record that many were not ready with the work assigned them. There is so very little required of each to make our meetings enjoyable if all are interested in the work that we feel constrained to urge upon every member as well as the little ones the necessity of giving some attention to it." A few years later, the Worthy Secretary snidely wrote that "during the long, tedious winter, a large number of our members have seemed to find their own firesides more pleasant than the grange." Entries from 1890 through 1896 bemoan the decline in membership and the deaths of many early Patrons.

Around the turn of the century, however, the Minnehaha got a second wind. Membership increased steadily until after World War I even as farm population declined. An entry from 1 May 1903 applauded the climbing membership numbers, and a hopeful discussion on 13 August 1908 suggested canvassing neighbors to draw members from their ranks. (Among the topics discussed frequently during these years were women's suffrage and restrictions on oleomargarine.) But by 1920 the Grange decided it had to solicit more outside renters for the hall just to make ends meet. Late that year, the chapter received a letter from the National Worthy Master "deploring conditions in Minnesota which would allow the decline of Grange spirit in the state" and chastising Minnesota for having only five organized subordinates. The minutes from 11 August 1923 grumble that "cooperation is all the trouble and if all members of the Grange cooperated better they would be able to do more."

The Great Depression and the Dust Bowl breathed life back into the Minnehaha. The first Golden Sheaf certificates (discussed in the preceding chapter) awarded in Minnesota went to Mr. and Mrs. George Millam—owners of the aforementioned Edina Mill—in

1933. The Grange hall building was moved in 1935; two years later, average attendance at meetings was up to 40. By the following year, membership totaled 107. The Grange apparently felt flush enough to solicit bids to redo the basement floor. Reflecting the ethnicity of the area, the four bidders bore the names of Carlson, Nelson, Jenson, and Anderson. The Minnehaha held a special meeting on 13 October 1941 to welcome Governor Harold E. Stassen and his wife as new members. On a more somber note, the members were urged a few years later to start locking the first-floor door to prevent pilfering of pocketbooks. By 1947, average attendance had climbed to 55 members per meeting.

The Minnehaha remained robust in the 1950s. During this decade, the chapter prided itself on maintaining the grave of Caroline Hall—Oliver Kelley's niece and a strong influence on the early Grange—and sponsoring a monument to her (fig. 4.2) in Minneapolis's Lakewood Cemetery. The ladies of the Minnehaha successfully petitioned to plant flowers on Miss Hall's grave on 15 May 1948 but were constrained to spend no more than $8. The minutes from 5 June 1954 record another outing to tend the grave. In 1950,

Figure 4.2. Monument to Caroline Hall, Lakewood Cemetery, Minneapolis. *Source:* Photograph by author

The Grange as a Fraternal, Educational, and Charitable Organization

the Minnehaha struggled to obtain permission from the National Grange to erect a suitable memorial, finally succeeding after nearly nine months.

Happily for me, the Worthy Secretary of the Minnehaha also began typing the minutes in 1950. Entries before that time are handwritten, and legibility is variable. The Patrons proudly printed up postcards for the national convention that year showing the building as the oldest Grange hall still in use, and it obtained the deed to the land surrounding the hall the following year. Brother George Willson was officially installed as "Water Boy" on 19 January 1952. He carried water to the hall each meeting for drinking and cooking until the Grange had sufficient funds to dig a well and buy a pump. On 3 June 1953, the Minnehaha obtained a mailing address: 5049 Normandale Road.

Much to both the Grangers' delight and mine, the minutes from 6 February 1954 report that members perused the old minutes from the late 1880s and found that "they talked about the same things we discuss today—the high cost of living, the drop in farm prices, how to get children up in the morning without calling [!] and the impossibility of growing alfalfa" north of the 40th parallel. A mysterious entry from 7 December 1957 crows that the Minnehaha Grange had become an honorary citizen of the state of Texas. Somewhat ominously, however, members had to start bringing in their own treats that year rather than relying on Grange funds to supply them.

The Minnehaha Grange hall fell on hard times in the mid-1960s, when a leak in the roof destroyed several items and heavy precipitation flooded the basement. Members apparently began slacking off as well—a March 1962 entry exhorts people to "cheerfully take turns serving lunch," and one from September of that year notes that "someone needs to destroy a bees' nest but no-one has volunteered." Two years later, the Worthy Secretary complained that "no-one has cut the grass." Membership was down everywhere in Minnesota in the 1960s, along with the farm population—only 235 Grangers attended the 1962 state convention.

Finances were tight as well—an entry from 18 May 1963 implores members to pay their dues, and one from 10 June 1964 laments that the chapter will have to borrow funds as its bank balance has dropped below $50. When the Minnesota Department of Transportation used the state's power of eminent domain to expand State Highway 100 through the Minnehaha's front yard, however, it forked over $14,500 to the chapter in 1968. Members refurbished the hall and moved it once again. But on 11 December 1970 a motion to restore more of the building failed. The Minnehaha merged with the Sunbeam and Crescent subordinates in 1971. The following year, the Minnehaha decided to remove its key from the Edina police office because unauthorized individuals were using it to enter the hall. By the mid-1970s, many members had fallen behind in paying their dues and were dropped from the rolls. The Minnehaha gave up its prized State Fair booth in 1973, the minutes became handwritten once more, and official meetings stopped in late 1978.

Today, only six active subordinates exist in the state of Minnesota. They are located centrally near St. Paul and Elk River (Elk River boasts the newest chapter, the Oliver Hudson Kelley, No. 834), in the south near Rochester and Stark, and in the northern section of the state near Mille Lacs in Aitkin and Nisswa. About 120 members statewide belong to the Grange.[6]

Membership and Finances

Funding a private voluntary organization is always a challenge. The Minnehaha Grange used a combination of dues, in-house activities, and transactions with outsiders to raise money. In terms of ready cash, the chapter rarely had more than $800. The one exception is just after it received payment from the Minnesota Department of Transportation in 1968.

Originally, monthly dues were 20 cents for men and 10 cents for women. Soon enough, however, the Minnehaha decided to equalize dues for all at 10 cents per month. But the chapter also had to pay dues to the State Grange out of its treasury. Correspondence from October 1949 records an increase in per capita state dues—from 25 cents quarterly to 35 cents. State quarterly dues had risen to 70 cents by 1954. By 1975, annual state dues were $5. The Minnehaha built in incentives for its members to pony up: on 5 February 1949, for instance, it requested dues of $2.90 per year but offered a 40 cent discount if Patrons paid before April 1.

Still, collection could be costly—and painful. A plaintive entry from 3 February 1951 notes that funds were quite low and members would like to raise dues but could not for fear that people would not pay higher rates. On 5 January 1952, the chapter agreed to send only one postcard out for dues because postage had doubled (to 2 cents). When the issue of delinquent dues began to generate considerable discussion in 1958, Grange members at first proposed individual visits to the miscreants but then decided to send committees instead. Dues collection became nearly impossible by the mid-1970s.

Raising money aside from dues was especially important after the Minnehaha built its own Grange hall. It faced typical maintenance expenses, including updating its facilities in July 1957 when a new village code required two toilets. The Grange began talking about installing electric lights in 1918 but had to wait for eight years after World War I ended to obtain them. Furnace and window repair were on the agenda on 21 November 1953, and the Patrons bought a new refrigerator on 21 May 1960.

The Minnehaha also spent money on entertainment items such as a player piano, a jukebox, and a record player with amplifier. Unfortunately, some unknown member used the jukebox inappropriately, jamming the records and damaging the needle.

The Minnehaha showed its patriotic side by purchasing a flagpole in 1928; it replaced the rope in 1956. Sadly, when members noted on 16 January 1965 that their flag had only 48 stars, they decided that funds were so short they would wait until the flag wore out before replacing it.

To meet expenses, the Minnehaha came up with clever ways to raise funds in-house. In 1921, it started the "penny march," renamed the "sunshine march" in 1949. At the end of each meeting, members stood up and marched around the room, dropping coins into a special box that helped fund the purchase of cards and flowers for sick and bereaved Brothers and Sisters. The Grange held its first "lumberjack dinner" (fig. 4.3) in 1938, where the men prepared and served a meal—much to the amusement of the women. In turn, the women sold quilts via a raffle. The proposed ticket price was $1 initially, but the Patrons shrewdly reduced it to 90 cents to avoid tax. In one innovative ploy, members in 1952 each took 25 cents from the treasury to "increase it" as they saw fit, then were supposed to bring all the

Lumberjack Night, 1948. *Source:* Minnesota Historical Society

proceeds back. Records do not indicate the success of this venture. In addition to raising funds via various tactics, the Minnehaha also saved money by collecting and disbursing coupons and gold bond stamps in the 1950s and '60s.

Specialized deals worked well for the Minnehaha. In 1949, it rented a television and charged viewers to watch Minnesota and Wisconsin football games. Via an arrangement with the telephone company in 1958, it installed a phone booth in front of the hall and obtained commissions when the booth made more than $10 a month. The minutes report that this was quite a successful enterprise for a time.

Renting out the Grange hall was also a lucrative business. The *Minnehaha Centennial History* (1973) states that the Grangers rented the hall from the very beginning, with renters including officials from the village of Edina. Members paid $10 for private parties in 1951, but outsiders paid more. The Grangers dithered about renting a room to an art instructor in 1959 and finally said yes. Despite its nonreligious nature, the Grange rented the hall to the Edina Methodist Church on 6 February 1960.

The minutes of the Minnehaha frequently mention rummage sales and paper drives.[7] In a reminder of the penny-pinching times of World War II, the Grange on 7 November 1942 proposed postponing a rummage sale "because of the gas and tire situation" but decided on 21 November to go ahead because gas rationing did not begin until 1 December. The minutes from 6 December 1942—the eve of the first anniversary of Pearl Harbor—celebrate a profit of $79.02. After a newspaper salvage sale brought in only $24.73 on 5 April 1952, however, the Minnehaha decided to abandon this less-than-effective means of raising money.

From the late 1930s to the late 1950s, the Minnehaha also sold metal sponges and plants, cookbooks, hand lotion, vanilla, advertising napkins, scrap iron and glass, ashtrays to fund preservation of the Kelley farm, and fertilizer.[8] A harbinger of the Minnehaha's financial woes in the early 1960s was its abortive attempt to sell lightbulbs. The idea was proposed on 21 January 1961, but increasingly desperate entries in the minutes suggest failure. An entry from 29 October says the sale was not going well. On 7 April 1962 the Grange decided to sell the bulbs at a reduced rate, and by 17 November 1962 members were urged to sell bulbs for anything above $1.

The All-Important Role of Education

The Minnehaha Grange, like subordinates throughout the country, devoted substantial portions of their meeting time to education. Sometimes the topic related closely to agricultural pursuits, but the Grangers also talked about school funding and curriculum, safety tips and fire prevention, other countries and cultures, and health. Minnehaha Patrons took seriously their duty to inform public officials about farm concerns as well as to state positions on such topics as whether all immigrants should read and write English, parents should pay for damages caused by minor children, Mainland China should be admitted to the United Nations, and restaurants should have to serve two different-sized portions.[9] (Incidentally, the answer to each was yes.)

Agricultural Education

Agricultural topics predominated in the first several decades for the Minnehaha Grange. Members listened to informational lectures on butter making, landscape gardening, fruit tree spraying, peppers, flax raising, chickens, the appropriate feed for dairy cattle, the proper care of apples, and jelly preservation.[10] The Patrons learned about the trees, fruits, fish, grains, and insects of Minnesota in a series of essays given from 1903 to 1905; later, they heard about how wood alcohol was saved from the waste of paper mills in Cloquet.[11] An employee of the State Department of Forest Conservation spoke in 1932 on the importance of taking caution with fire and, not surprisingly, conserving forests. In the 1950s, the Minnehaha hosted discussions of the nutritional value of onions and the benefits of wheat free from stem rust infection.[12]

But the Minnehaha Grangers also learned about agricultural practices elsewhere. Brother Millman spoke in 1909 of his experience with eucalyptus and India rubber trees. Other members discussed the poultry industry in California, various types of cacti, and a swine project in Guatemala.[13]

Lively debates among members took place, too, just as Ignatius Donnelly had hoped. Was wheat or corn more profitable? How about black or red raspberries? What about cows, hogs, or chickens? And what were the most profitable breeds of chicken, anyway? An 1883 discussion of whether raising root vegetables to feed stock or depending on mill feed made more economic sense was resolved in favor of roots. (A follow-up discussion on whether dancing should be allowed in the Grange hall came to no conclusion.) Members decided that market gardening—small-scale production of fruits and vegetables—could pay better than the farming of grains and other crops but would force them to get up earlier. The location or quality of soil had no effect on the severity of potato rot. And the more one cultivated in dry weather, the better the soil retained moisture. Left unresolved was whether one eye or two was better in a potato, and whether farmers should manure before plowing or after the crop was up. The Minnehaha Grangers discussed the grading of wheat, the merits of feeding cattle more grain and less hay because the price of hay was so high, and the benefits of higher butter fat in ice cream.[14]

The chapter also complained that public schools did not pay enough attention to agriculture, and so it offered suggestions for improvement to rural schools.[15] This matter concerned southern Granges as well, which advocated for more practical classes in the public schools. Mississippi Grangers were concerned about overreliance on cotton and wanted better scientific knowledge taught in schools. At first, however, they opposed using taxes to help fund this—particularly for black schools—but some eventually relented. Washington farmers similarly wanted improved education but didn't want to pay for frequent updates in textbooks. Texas Grangers also agitated for improved vocational education.[16] National Worthy Master Aaron Jones publicly supported better rural education in an interview he gave in April 1900 to the *Grand Rapids (MI) Herald*.

Each year, the Minnehaha Patrons set up a booth at the state fair to educate the public about different aspects of farming. Figure 4.4 shows the exhibit from 1948. They discussed hogs in 1950 and insecticides in 1972. They won the sweepstakes for their display on tomatoes in 1953, and two years later took home a blue ribbon for their presentation on onions. The minutes from 4 September 1965 report a red ribbon received but complain about inconsistency in the judging. The 1969 display on car pollution generated judges' comments that the Grangers needed to include more facts.

Figure 4.4. Minnehaha Grange State Fair Booth, 1948. *Source:* Minnesota Historical Society

Minnehaha Grangers were convinced of the importance of the agricultural education provided by the University of Minnesota. An animated discussion of Edward H. Faulkner's *Plowman's Folly* (1943) noted that the University Farm did not agree with the plowing recommended in the book. Early in their existence, the Minnehaha Patrons passed a resolution asking for an appropriation of $16,000 to use at an experimental farm.[17] Elsewhere, Grangers encouraged better allocation of funding under the Morrill Act of 1862 (which established land-grant colleges across the United States), helped found Mississippi State College at Starkville, and supported Texas A&M.[18]

The Minnehaha Grangers were concerned about gender equity at the University of Minnesota. The minutes for 2 February 1896 state that it had "long been promised that at the earliest possible moment, Girls should be admitted to the school." Yet "such promise has never been fulfilled." So the members of the Grange and the women of Minnesota "most respectfully and urgently request[ed]" the legislature to appropriate funding to build accommodations for the girls. Mississippi Grangers took another approach for educating females: in 1884, they supported the establishment of the Industrial Institute and College for Women to teach sewing, stenography, and teacher training.[19]

General Education

The Minnehaha, like other subordinates, aimed to promote improvements in public schooling as well as to educate its members generally. Mary Ann Mayo of Michigan, a leading Grange figure, urged farm women to avoid drudgery and read books—doing so would increase their knowledge of chemistry and botany, she claimed.[20] Worthy Master Sarah Baird, in her early twentieth-century speech to the Minnesota State Grange, saw another angle: she thought school buildings should be used in the evenings for community gatherings, although she also thought that "school boards were too narrow-minded" to permit this practice. Baird's speech also favored funding for vocational education.

Educational funding continued to occupy the Minnehaha Grangers in later decades. On 7 May 1938, Sister Vinson requested the formation of a committee to decide whether the Minnehaha should urge Minnesota's US senators, Henrik Shipstead and Ernest Lundeen, to support bill S419 on Federal Aid for Education. (In a not-so-playful aside, Sister Olin suggested writing the senators to ask them instead to reduce federal spending overall.)[21] Education is front and center in a resolution adopted 6 September 1947: "We think the shortage of teachers for public schools is a national calamity. We are worried that teachers are paid less than janitors, and we think this is why they are leaving. So we want the Minnesota State Grange to take this to the National Grange to draw nationwide attention to this deplorable condition." In the 1970s, the Minnehaha voted to beef up school milk and lunch programs, but opposed busing of children to integrate public schools and using tax revenue to finance nonpublic schools. Today's National Grange website calls for improved educational quality, particularly in rural areas.[22]

Running a subordinate was an education in itself. Buying supplies for the Grange sharpened budgeting know-how. The parliamentary nature of the meetings helped educate farmers in the ways of public life; the emphasis on discussion and participation cultivated public-speaking skills among members, including women. An entry for 21 November 1964 encouraged everyone to develop a good public-speaking voice; on 6 April 1968, a member read a paper she was planning to present in a Dale Carnegie contest. Studies of subordinate Granges in Washington, Mississippi, and Alabama report a similar emphasis on public speaking. One Grange scholar refers to women in particular honing their public-speaking skills in Grange meetings.[23]

Some Grange meetings tackled basic home and gardening skills. Minnehaha Grangers heard lectures on labor-saving devices for the kitchen, the history and background of hooked rugs, soil-less gardens, herbs and their uses, lawns and shrubs, Victory gardens, upkeep of electrical appliances and pressure cookers, salad making, care of house plants, and horticulture.[24] Sarah Baird's speech to the Minnesota State Grange in the early twentieth century praised Mrs. Ellen M. Richards for founding the National Home Economics Association and establishing the *Journal of Home Economics*.

The nature of family interactions sparked conversations as well. On 16 January 1909, Brother Lind "told what part the husband played in making a happy home. His ideas were good. If his suggestions were more generally followed there would be fewer unhappy homes." Spiritual training in the home was the topic for 4 June 1938.

The Patrons also displayed interest in science, technology, history, and economics. They heard papers on "What is Asbestus [sic]?," the Boulder Dam, chemistry, different kinds of ammunition, semi-precious gems of Minnesota, silver, and "If we landed on the moon, what would we say?" They had an unsuccessful demonstration of the radio, a more successful demonstration of the uses of aluminum, and a tour of a bomb shelter.[25] On 1 May 1948, Sister Archer had the distinction of being one of the first members to see a television broadcast—a baseball game shown on a TV set at Dayton's department store. Despite the earlier malfunction with the radio, Minnehaha Grangers suggested using it as a means of teaching current history via broadcasts from the United Nations. In 1943, veterans of World War I talked about where they were on Armistice Day; fifteen years later, the Patrons heard a program on a pioneer girls' boarding school. Early in the Grange's existence, a member "read an article from the *Chicago Express* entitled United States Bonds, representing them as one of the greatest frauds ever practiced on the people."[26] On 3 October 1959, the Minnehaha hosted a guest psychologist who spoke about a workshop that gave mentally disabled people the ability to make a living.

Safety was a big concern, as was health. The Grangers learned about auto safety, discussed the terrible death toll on highways and the merits of ghost cars (unmarked police cars), and heard lectures about drunken drivers. In the 1940s, the Grangers conversed about glass and nails in the street and decided to contact schools to ask them to teach children their civic duty in keeping streets clean; members also were urged to listen to broadcasts about juvenile delinquency. They celebrated in May 1961 when the Worthy State Lecturer received an award from the governor for her efforts in stressing highway safety. Six people representing the ghosts of those who died in accidents put on a safety skit in 1964, with each telling how he or she had perished because of carelessness with electricity. Fire prevention was the topic on at least two occasions.[27] After a talk on emergency first aid by the Edina police in 1960, the Minnehaha Grangers decided to run a free Red Cross first-aid class. Health issues covered in the early 1960s included how much strontium appeared in milk, how to recognize tuberculosis in a person, and how to protect oneself from disease by drinking milk. The Patrons also heard lectures about Alcoholics Anonymous, the Arthritis and Rheumatism Foundation, and the US Department of Agriculture.[28]

Literary and cultural issues also made appearances at Minnehaha meetings. In 1894, members took turns bringing in six uncommon English words to teach their pronunciation and meaning. Half a century later, the state home economics chair urged members to "read only worthwhile literature and attend good movies." The chapter set aside funds to buy a set of encyclopedias and even agreed to pay for Sister McNeil's courses on world leadership, dramatics, and recreation at the University of Minnesota. In the 1940s, Peter Olson came to teach folk dancing, and a lecturer informed the Minnehaha chapter about the Indians at Hudson Bay. In February 1949, everyone read his or her favorite poem.[29] This tradition continues in the Granges of today, which sponsor competitions and activities in music, art, public speaking, and crafts.[30]

The Minnehaha Grangers learned about international topics as well. In 1902, "Sister Baird read from the history of the great Boer War, telling of the great wealth of South Africa, particularly in the Gold mines of the Transvaal region over which there has been so much contention, and that this wealth is the principle [sic] cause of the long protracted war there." Three years later, members heard a paper on "Porto [sic] Rico, giving some of the habbits [sic] and peculiarities of the Natives." Members watched a movie of "scenic Norway," heard about a literary program in Israel and a general labor strike in Finland in the 1950s, discussed the St. Lawrence Seaway, enjoyed a lecture hour on travel to England and Europe, and saw slides in 1966 from an African safari and from Brasilia.[31] The Minnehaha Grangers invited two Japanese Americans to speak to the group on 7 April 1945 (four months before V-J Day), an Arab American on 19 April 1958 (just after the Suez crisis), and Indian farmers on 3 June 1961 (shortly before the Green Revolution transformed Indian agriculture).

Educating the Legislature

Like other subordinates, the Minnehaha saw a duty to inform the legislature about its position on farming and education as well as a variety of other concerns. Although the impact of their resolutions and suggestions is unclear, their positions tell us much about what this Grange saw as important policy issues.

Women's suffrage occupied the Grange in the early years. On 6 February 1886, the Minnehaha decided to open the next meeting to "admit outsiders to listen to a discussion on Women's Suffrage [*sic*]." Although both sides "ably discussed" the issue, bad weather unfortunately led to a very small turnout. Patrons also listened to a lecture about Susan B. Anthony on 17 September 1904. Suffrage was an issue that occupied other Granges as well. Apparently due to some vocal women at the meeting, the Indiana State Grange adopted equal suffrage resolutions in 1881 and 1892. The National Grange came out for suffrage in 1885 but reverted to supporting state rights to establish policy in 1886. It finally decided to back the suffrage amendment in 1915.[32]

Oleomargarine raised the early Minnehaha's hackles. The Oleomargarine Act of 1886—which pitted dairy interests against corn growers and livestock groups—imposed a tax of 0.25 percent on margarine not colored yellow and of 10 percent on yellow margarine. On 18 February 1888, the Minnehaha Grange adopted and forwarded to their congressmen Brother McCabe's resolution demanding that they vote against repeal of the act: "Whereas it is now certain that the Cattlemen of the Plains and the Manufacturers of Oleo Margarine will make a desperate attempt to secure the repeal of the Oleomargarine Law to enable them to again flood the market unrestrained; with Bogus Butter to the ruin of the dairy interests of the Country. Be it therefore resolved that We demand of our Senators and Representatives that they stand by the interest of their constituents and the causes of common honesty, and resist by all honorable means the repeal of Said Law, and endeavor if possible to make the law against fraud a more effective and more thorough protection to the honest products of the dairy." A speech by Worthy Master Sarah Baird to the State Grange a quarter-century later reiterated this charge to the legislators of her day. Minnesota did not lift restrictions on margarine until 1963; it took Wisconsin—the predominant milk-producing state at the time—another four years.[33]

Baird's speech also took up other issues. The Patrons supported direct election of senators, opposed the shipment of alcohol into dry territory, and asked that widows receive pensions that would allow them to keep all their children together. Around this time, the Minnehaha Grange on 19 August 1911 indicated its support for reciprocity with Canada in the matter of tariff reductions and free trade.

The Minnehaha took pride in the fact that Franklin Delano Roosevelt was the first Granger to become president. On 18 March 1933, it wired FDR the news that it had "passed a resolution wishing you every success for your administration and more power in your efforts in our present distress. To that end we have tonight wired our Senators to support you in your economy program." The Patrons had indeed done so, criticizing Senator Shipstead because he "did not back up the President in his emergency bank bill. We demand you support him in his efforts to maintain the credit of the Nation by voting for the economy bill today and further serve your constitutancy [sic] by voting to give the President the emergency powers he asks." It sent the same message to Senator Thomas Schall (who had supported the bank bill) without the first sentence.[34]

FDR's large programs were not the only concern for the Minnehaha and other Granges during the tough years of the 1930s. The Minnesota State Grange in 1933 opposed a general sales tax, favored a tax on radio stations and an income tax (to replace some of the burden of the tax on real estate), and wanted stability for the dollar. It also favored conservation of natural resources and prohibition of hunting without obtaining the landowner's permission, but it opposed wholesale drainage of swamps and liquor traffic of any form.

Later in the decade, the Minnehaha took up the question of consumer information. On 2 February 1937, it proposed organizing a Hennepin County Consumers' Institute that would serve as a "united front against monopoly and price fixing" and would offer plainly worded grading and labeling information on products.

The resolutions adopted in the 1940s offer a nice mix of national and local concerns. On 7 September 1940, the Minnehaha resolved that national defense was necessary but wanted to defer conscription until the country tried a volunteer army. In the same resolution, it stated, "We think the state grange should do something about all the liberation of Chinese pheasants which are destroying market gardens.... It should trap and ship them to more open places in the state." On 6 September 1947, the Patrons thanked Governor Luther Youngdahl for his opposition to gambling and slot machines. The Grange supported Youngdahl's bills to ban both.

In 1954, the Grangers who attended the Corn States Grange Lecturers conference discussed the possibility of lowering tariff rates. They also acknowledged that the US price support system was one factor in causing them to lose some foreign markets, and they floated the possibility of moving to a dual system that charged one price to foreigners and another to US residents.

The resolutions for the 1960s cover topics from juvenile delinquency to gun control. The resolutions adopted on 3 March 1962 opposed strict work practices (also known as featherbedding)—thus conflicting with the desires of industrial unions—and supported building a sound public opinion of the farmer. The resolution sent to the Minnesota state legislature on 7 September 1968 asked that candidates have party designations, parents pay for damages from vandalism caused by their minor children and appear in police stations and courts to pick up their children, and government eliminate deficit spending and enforce criminal laws more stringently. The Grange also went on record opposing gun regulation, apparently fearing the possibility of firearm confiscation.

Resolutions from the 1970s are even more far-ranging and reflect the graying, increasingly conservative nature of the Minnehaha. On 2 June 1972, the Grange voted to support the family farm and cancel welfare benefits to able-bodied persons who refused employment. It opposed furnishing welfare payments to strikers, transferring of highway tax revenue to any other transport, banning pesticides before doing thorough research on their effects, and allowing college students to vote in towns where they temporarily resided. On 15 September 1974, it urged the president, Congress, governor, and state representatives to keep a lid on wages for unionized labor because "the rate of inflation is hurting us all." It also requested that the permitted blood alcohol level for drivers be reduced.[35] On 1 March 1975, when the Minnehaha's roster included only a few aged members, the chapter supported the State Grange recommendation that government enforce uniform bumper height regulations, retain the 55 mph speed limit, support reduction of the legal alcohol limit, and permit states to be in charge of land use.

The October resolution from that same year stated: "Whereas we are now more concerned than ever before with not wasting food, and whereas the restaurants usually serve larger portions of meat than the average adult can consume, be it resolved that the restaurants, on their meat menus, have two different portions, priced accordingly. . . . This would help curtail uneaten portions ending up in the garbage pail and be a boost to our economy in two ways—people could afford to eat out oftener and less food would be wasted."

The Minnehaha's interest in legislative reform is reflected in actions taken by today's National Grange. The National Grange website reports that it wants to protect solid prosperity for family farmers and promote effective immigration reform. It calls for improved and expanded telecom service, health care, public safety, transportation, civic participation, and sustainable energy in rural areas. It also expresses concern about the impact of financial crises on rural areas. To assure a "competitive and efficient farm service," it advocates the elimination of direct government farm programs. The National Grange also conducts an annual two-day fly-in to Washington, DC, to visit members of Congress. In spring 2013, twenty-three Grangers traveled to hear Representative Collin Peterson (D-MN) talk about the pending farm bill.[36]

Some of today's State Granges are also active in certain legislative areas. Washington appears to be the largest Grange with about 50,000 members; its main concern is water use and conservation. The same is true for California, although its Grange is only about a quarter the size of Washington's. In October 2014, the California Grange called for a ban on fracking, which is allegedly polluting the state's aquifers. Pennsylvania's Grange is also concerned about water, but in a different way—it focuses on flood control. New York's Grange is quite vocal in its stance against unfunded mandates. It wants to halt illegal immigration but to make hiring legal migrants easier. It also supports importing prescription drugs from Canada. The Michigan Grange advocates a number of agricultural programs, including favorable tax treatment for farmers; it also stresses respect for the flag. The New Hampshire Grange, with its seventy-five subordinates, is strongly against animal cruelty and genetically modified organisms.[37]

Charitable and Community Service

In the early years, the Minnehaha focused its charitable efforts on helping those who had suffered through a natural disaster. In 1874, it donated funds to persons who had endured massive grasshopper plagues. The Patrons collected clothing and made sheets and comforters for the residents of neighboring St. Louis Park who lost everything in a 1904 tornado.[38] They raised $41 for the victims of the 1906 San Francisco earthquake and fire.

World War II and its aftermath inspired the Minnehaha to contribute blood, funds, goods, and time. Members donated blood in the name of the Grange on several occasions. Early on, the Minnehaha gave a total of $15 to be split among the Red Cross, the Salvation Army, and the USO. A card party that raised $37 in 1943 was divided between soldiers and the Red Cross. The Patrons gave bundles for Britain, sent sweets and pajamas to soldiers, collected milkweed to stuff life jackets, and made surgical dressings and handcrafted items. Grange members did 126 hours of sewing for the Red Cross in March 1944 and 236 hours in January 1945. When airplane spotting required 106 volunteers, Minnehaha Grangers stepped forward, saying that "every Granger was 100 percent American and could be called on at any time to fulfill this duty."[39]

After the war, the National Grange put sixty young German immigrants to work on Grange farms and contributed food and other items to war-torn Europe. The Minnehaha sent a check to CARE for needy Europeans, $10 for food and $5 in unrestricted cash to the Red Cross, $6.55 to Radio Free Europe, and $2 to Greece to purchase two sewing machines.[40]

Charity did not end after World War II with Europe. The Minnehaha sent mittens to Korea in the 1950s, money and yarn to Algeria in the early 1960s, and care packages to the soldiers in Vietnam in 1969.[41]

Minnehaha Patrons also looked out for veterans at the local VA hospital. In the late 1960s and early 1970s, they sent lap robes and bibs, lemonade and cookies, rugs, bed socks, dining room chairs, slippers, cab fare to attend Twins baseball games, Easter baskets, money for the servicemen's club at the airport, and grocery coupons.[42]

Children, the poor, and Native Americans also received contributions from the Minnehaha Grangers. The Patrons collected toys, milk, and blankets for "unfortunate children in Faribault" and elsewhere, clothing for the Children's Mission as well as $10 to replace a stolen public-address system, clothing for the Children's Home at Lake Owasso in St. Paul, and $50 for the Bar-None Ranch for Boys. Fifteen dollars went for Christmas food baskets for the needy in 1959; later contributed were 65 pairs of eyeglasses, several boxes of books, and clothing. An "Indian named Mrs. Skinaway from Macgregor" thanked the chapter for clothing in 1948; calls were put out for a "layette for an Indian girl" and "Christmas gifts for Indian mission kids in Onamia" in the mid-1950s; flannel blankets were donated for "Indian relief" in 1962; and clothing and food went to the Little Flower Indian Mission in Mille Lacs throughout the 1960s.[43]

Health and safety issues also concerned the Minnehaha Grangers. They raised a crop of flax to buy an ambulance for the city of Edina in 1948, and they picked up glass along the highway in 1950. They contributed funds to the Georgia Warm Springs Foundation, the polio fund, the Hennepin County Tuberculosis Society, the Cambridge mental hospital, the Fraser School for the Retarded, and Camp Courage. The Minnehaha Grangers made identification buttons for heart-attack victims and donated sheets for cancer dressings and lap robes for cancer patients.[44] Instead of holding a "sunshine penny march" on 16 January 1960, the group sponsored a "dime march" and sent the proceeds to the March of Dimes.

The Minnehaha also took care of its members and gave back to the community. Grangers contributed blood for members of their own chapter as well as to a "Grange girl" in South Dakota. They frequently sent flowers and cards to the sick and bereaved among their members, and they gave $2 to the National Grange Youth Leadership Training fund. The Grangers donated money to the building fund of the Edina Covenant Church and, to be fair, also sent a (smaller) contribution to the Normandale Lutheran Church. They hosted a dinner of appreciation for Edina firefighters in battling a 400-acre brush fire in 1954, and they built an outdoor fireplace at the park next to the Grange hall a year later (hopefully with the blessing of the Edina Fire Department).[45]

Many of today's State Granges perform similar sorts of community service projects and highlight them on their websites. The Massachusetts Grange takes pride in its projects for the deaf, for instance, and the Illinois Grange stresses programs providing pregnancy care and the promotion of information about autism.[46] The newest Grange in Minnesota, the "Oliver Hudson Kelley" (No. 834, established in Elk River in October 2012), focuses its efforts on urban micro-farming, heirloom gardening, and community activities such as a book club, a lecture series focused on Grange history, and exhibitions of town ball (a nineteenth-century precursor of modern baseball).[47]

Fraternization

The pages of the Minnehaha Grange minute books are filled with references to holiday parties, dinners, and dances; cards, bingo, and bunco playing; skits, tableaux, and carnivals; singing, picnics, and patriotic programs.[48] Parades were popular, as figure 4.5 suggests. Theme parties were all the rage, with a Hawaiian evening on 19 January 1963 and what the Grangers called a "poverty party" on 5 February 1965. ("Poverty parties" were somewhat dubious gatherings where attendees dressed shabbily and consumed cheap food and drink.) On 4 February 1928, "It was then suggested that a Poverty social be put on for next time but we found we were going to be so poverty stricken . . . it would be too true to be comfortable."

Unique entertainment showed up in the Minnehaha Grange hall. On 31 October 1881, "Master Charles Gancy entertained the audience [*sic*] with his rehearsal of April-fool day—which was

Figure 4.5 Parade Float, Minnehaha Grange, 1947. *Source:* Minnesota Historical Society

The Grange as a Fraternal, Educational, and Charitable Organization

comical in itself and much more so when rendered by our comical Charly." The Grangers were much amused in 1913 at "the dexterity of certain brothers in attempting to pick up a dollar from the floor with their feet." A "cleverly presented" debate over whether "our wise cracks are wiser than yours" occurred on 5 March 1938. Figures 4.6 and 4.7 portray a switch in traditional gender roles at the 1947 picnic. In 1961, Patrons held a contest to see how many odd objects could be found in women's purses. In an unpalatable example from 1927 that illustrates the casual racism of the era, "the serving brothers turned themselves into colored waiters, with cap and jacket and ebony faces. Much fun was enjoyed."

But Grangers weren't simply left to their own devices for entertainment. They could turn to useful instructional booklets such as the *Heap O' Joy Grange Lecturers' Book and Booster Night Programs,* which contained plays, recitations, pantomimes, tableaux, stunts, and songs. This manual urged Patrons that "your aim on Booster Night is to gain new members" but reminded them not to "stress too much the financial benefits which may accrue to new members."[49]

Figure 4.6. Ladies' Nail-Driving Contest, 1947. *Source:* Minnesota Historical Society

Men's Needle-Threading Contest, 1947. *Source:* Minnesota Historical Society

Patriotism was emphasized at the Minnehaha's meetings. Everyone was urged to vote on 2 November 1940, for example. These Patrons unanimously decided to restore the pledge of allegiance as part of their regular meetings on 21 October 1961, even though the commissioner of protocol in Washington, DC, had given permission to omit it.

Two intriguing entries from the early years suggest that fraternization did not always take the appropriate form. On 18 March 1876, the Grange "moved that charges be prefered [*sic*] against Bro. Frank Edgerly & drawn in proper form for the trial for said Bro. at our

The Grange as a Fraternal, Educational, and Charitable Organization 91

next Regular meeting." And, on 20 April 1883, "a very grave charge against Wm Ewing by Mary Hawks was read and a committee appointed of three to investigate and try the case." The minutes do not reveal the nature of the charges nor the character of their disposition.

Summing Up

The records from the Minnehaha Grange (Minnesota No. 398) provide an extraordinarily comprehensive picture of life in a typical subordinate. The longevity of this organization and the detailed nature of its minutes give us more than a glimpse of the joys and trials of a private, voluntary enterprise. Because the Minnehaha survived for so long, its records confirm that the 1879 vision set forth by Jonathan Woodman of a social and fraternal Grange persisted for the next century of the Patrons' existence.

What appears in the Minnehaha minutes of their biweekly meetings and in other documents is an account of a group of people brought together by agricultural concerns striving to create a welcoming and social atmosphere for its members. But it also furnishes a picture of an enterprise that took seriously its role in providing educational opportunities, representing farm interests to legislative bodies, and offering meaningful service to the larger community. Its demise is a familiar, bittersweet one in an era where "bowling alone" seems to prevail.[50]

5

Legacies of the Grange
*Its Influence on Grassroots Organizations
and American Law*

> We desire a proper equality, equity, and fairness, protection for the weak, restraint upon the strong; in short, justly distributed burdens and justly distributed power. These are American ideas, the very essence of American independence.
>
> —*Declaration of Purposes of the Patrons of Husbandry*

The Grange movement was an experiment in cooperation that "arouse[d farmers] from apathy" and helped the country heal after the Civil War. In keeping with Oliver Kelley's desire to create a national agricultural brotherhood, the first major postbellum national convention held in the South was the Granger gathering in Charleston in 1875.[1]

But the Grange did more than bring farmers together for social and educational purposes. It serves as an excellent example of how collective action can succeed—and how it might fail. The Grangers' method of operation influenced other farmer associations, organizations like the Knights of Labor, and, at least indirectly, modern movements such as Occupy Wall Street. The Grange, like these other groups, calls attention to how the fruits of economic success are distributed.[2]

The Patrons of Husbandry also raised two important political economy questions: (1) What is the role of the government in regulating private enterprise and restricting private property rights when public interest may be at stake? (2) What part should the judiciary play in reviewing the actions of legislatures and the regulatory bodies they establish? These are ongoing issues, cropping up everywhere from labor-market restrictions and civil rights to health care and the environment. Although the Grange is now a relatively small rural fraternal association, its influence on America's postbellum public policy and jurisprudence is significant.

The Grange and Collective Action

The Grange is a prime example of the power of a grassroots organization in determining economic outcomes for its members. It caused the concentrated forces on the other side of the market to sit up and take notice. In many respects, however, it revealed how its efforts to form its own power base and eradicate the middleman could generate scorn and failure as well as nervous attention by opponents.

The Grange showed farmers they could unite for a cause, and it constructed a pattern for later farm organizations with its use of paid recruiters, its emphasis on education, and its inclusion of women.[3] The Grange was a strong supporter of the Department of Agriculture, which was elevated to cabinet status in 1889 and remains one of the largest civilian federal agencies.[4] The Patrons enjoyed considerable success for many years in hamstringing margarine producers, even helping obtain legislation to color margarine pink in an effort to make it look unpalatable.[5] Grange activism in countering railroad power by agitating for better water navigation helped build the wing dams that line the Mississippi River today. Grange insurance and utility cooperatives continue to flourish, although they now also serve people who are not part of the Grange.

Yet its often-unsuccessful experiments with economic cooperation showed the Grange that middlemen could indeed serve a useful function rather than simply act as unnecessary, costly parasites. Its effort to force Cyrus McCormick to accept Grange-appointed agents caused McCormick to sputter "[This] request . . . smacks strongly of the Mormon rule of business. . . . Any candid, thinking farmer will see on a moment's reflection that we not only have the right, but for our own protection must select as our agents the men we find best qualified to sell our machines."[6] Aside from his religious slight—presumably, he was referring to a perception that Mormons did business only with others of their faith—McCormick had a fair point. The Grangers were free to set up their own business if they didn't like how McCormick ran his—but when they went into harvester manufacture in Iowa, for example, they failed miserably.

Grange enterprises also failed when the benefits from defecting from a cooperative arrangement exceeded the benefits of remaining faithful. For large numbers of individual farmers, withholding products from market to keep prices up simply was not feasible—milk could spoil and crops left in the field could rot. Harvested crops could often be stored, but equally often the lure of immediate profit was too hard to resist, especially for small farmers. The Rochdale plan under which many Grange cooperatives operated had particular drawbacks for capital-hungry farmers: in good years farmers wanted distribution of profits rather than retention and re-capitalization, but in bad years they were reluctant to adhere to the cash-only rule, which was absolutely necessary for enterprises already operating on a shoestring.

Farmers even found that alleged enemies could sometimes be allies. In an ironic example, the Washington State Grangers wanted to send delegates to a political demonstration in 1909, so they requested that the Northern Pacific and Bellingham Bay & British Columbia railroads run special trains so that the farmers could get to the meeting on time.[7] Oliver Kelley's part ownership of a proposed Florida railroad (mentioned in the introduction) is another case in point.

Some of what farmers learned from the Grange is what NOT to do. Coalitions fall apart when they do not deliver what they promise, when members stretch beyond their skills and expertise, when defection is too great, or when they do not successfully align themselves with like-minded, politically powerful entities. One scholar suggests that the largest lesson learned by farmers from the Grange experience is that no one panacea will solve everyone's problems.[8]

Cooperatives with small numbers of individuals with common interests—like today's cheese, ethanol, sugar beet, and dairy associations that include processors and distributors as well as farmers—have had more success in gaining economic and political influence than the sprawling Grange. The Farm Bureau has had notable staying power in part because it teamed up with agricultural extension services located in land-grant universities. Although the Grange emphasized agricultural education, it did not cultivate close connections with large public enterprises.

Yet the Grange offers more than a cautionary tale to farmers about what might work and what might not work. The Grange's declaration of purposes resonates strongly in a similar document (*A Declaration of Principles*) put forth by the Knights of Labor. Grangers influenced at least two political movements: the Anti-Monopoly Party established in 1884 and led by Ignatius Donnelly, and the People's Party organized in 1891. The platform for the Anti-Monopoly Party supported maximum-hours legislation; it opposed monopolies of wood and coal, extravagant salaries, and protective tariffs on manufactures. Although the Anti-Monopoly Party lasted for only one election, it helped give rise to the Farmer-Labor and then the DFL (Democratic-*Farmer*-Labor) party in Minnesota.[9] The People's Party's best-known endorsement went to William Jennings Bryan, whose "Cross of Gold" speech at the 1896 Democratic National Convention contrasted the hardworking farmer with the speculative big-city businessman.

One might even view the Occupy Wall Street movement and its spin-offs as modern-day examples of Grange-like enterprises. In its first incarnation, Occupy Wall Street comprised loose groups of young people angry with the financial system but lacking in focus and policy proposals. Its rage gave it a lot of press, but its inability to articulate a clear position meant the movement had no real clout. A disorganized celebration of its one-year anniversary generated bitter complaints about disregard for those trying to get to work through the chaotic streets and produced a loss of public support. Yet the idea of a grassroots organization concerned about concentrations of wealth and power struck a chord with many, and led to tighter, more focused, and arguably more successful groups like Occupy Bank, Occupy the SEC, and Occupy Sandy.[10]

The Grange and American Law

The nineteenth-century Granger laws and Granger cases bring up important questions about the nature and treatment of goods and services that may have a "public interest" component. In the Granger case of *Munn v. Illinois,* Chief Justice Morrison Waite relied on English law to find that, when private property was affected with a public interest, the owner was not free to do whatever he wished with it.[11] Justice Waite went on to say that "property does become clothed with a public interest when used in a manner to make it of public consequence and affect the community at large. When, therefore, one devotes his property to a use in which the public has an interest, he, in effect, grants to the public an interest in that use, and must submit to be controlled by the public for the common good."

The court determined in *Munn* and related cases that grain warehouses and railroads were "clothed with a public interest." Two features of these enterprises seemed to compel the judges: they were open for use to anyone who paid for them, and they commanded near-monopoly of the service provided. To the court's eye, this left customers with an unpalatable choice: pay what the company asked, or go without. Because the demand for rail transport over short distances was small relative to the capital investment required to establish a railroad, in many areas a single road was sufficient to supply the needs of potential patrons. Additional roads were unlikely to enter the market, even if the existing road charged monopoly prices. Potential competition thus did not serve to curb a company's power in these sorts of industries, at least for short hauls. The *Munn* court therefore upheld the right of states to regulate rates charged by privately owned companies that provided a good or service—like transportation and warehousing—that was "clothed with a public interest."

Some view this sort of regulation as interference with private property rights. The plaintiffs in *Munn* and related cases argued that the Granger statutes deprived them of private property without due process of law, thus violating the recently enacted Fourteenth Amendment. They should be free, they reasoned, to set whatever rates they wished and would presumably set them to maximize the value of the company. Supreme Court Justice Stephen Field dissented in *Munn,* saying that the regulation of compensation for the use of private property was not within the scope of a state's police power.

Others celebrate the outcome of *Munn.* Some consider regulation as a reasonable alternative to state confiscation of utilities and common carriers. Others, like Wisconsin Senator Robert La Follette, see monopoly pricing as unfair and think governments should be able to regulate prices to protect consumers.[12] Both reinforce their positions by pointing to the substantial land grants, tax breaks, and financial aid extended to railroads. In their opinion, if railroads benefited from public largesse, they should also submit to public oversight. Field's position that railroad property is purely private neglects the crucial historical role of the public sector in establishing rail transportation across the United States.

Opponents of *Munn* question whether regulation as practiced actually enhances consumer welfare. In one view, railroad regulation not only takes away from companies but also fails to benefit customers. In yet a different view, regulation is generally seen as working to the benefit of the regulated industry.[13] This "capture theory" of regulation is appealing to many mainstream economists. The benefits of regulation friendly to an industry are highly concentrated, whereas the costs to consumers are highly dispersed. No one has a greater financial stake in influencing the regulatory process than the members of the regulated industry itself.

This conflict in viewpoints has yet to be resolved in the law. The following sections discuss how the Granger laws and Granger cases have influenced both transportation law and the laws governing other commodities and activities. One important concern is the role of regulation. A second is the procedure by which regulation is implemented; in particular, what are the appropriate responsibilities for legislatures and the judiciary?

Transportation Law

Worthy Master Herschel Newsom, in his address at the 100th annual convention of the National Grange, lauded the organization's actions in shaping the laws governing US transportation:

> The Grange, throughout its entire life, has directed much of its efforts toward the development of a sound transportation policy. . . . Railroads grew more powerful to the point that abuses against the shippers and general public were becoming rampant. It was then that the famous Grange Laws . . . were passed. . . . They led to the creation in 1887 of the Interstate Commerce Commission. . . . The next major development in the field of transportation regulation occurred in 1935 with the passage of the Federal Motor Carrier Act. Here, again, the Grange stepped into the picture by demanding that haulers of Agricultural products be exempted from regulation by the ICC. . . . The Grange led the drive to "get farmers out of the mud." It supported passage of the 1916 Federal Aid Highway Act . . . [and the] 1921 Federal Aid Highway Act. . . . Toward the end of 1944 . . . at the insistence of the Grange, a secondary farm-to-market road system was designated and became eligible for fifty percent federal funds support, as had been true of federal primary roads since 1921. . . . In 1956, a great program was developed and approved by Congress, with vigorous Grange support, to build a 41,000 mile Interstate Highway System.[14]

Although Newsom may overstate the Grange's influence a bit, it is nonetheless true that the Granger laws heralded legal developments that grew up alongside the modern methods of transport that crisscross the country.

Chapter 2 discussed the Granger laws and mentioned the 1886 case of *Wabash, St. Louis, and Pacific Railway Company v. Illinois*, which negated the *Munn* provision that states could regulate interstate commerce that affected their own citizens. Under the commerce clause of the US Constitution, only the US Congress can regulate interstate commerce; under the landmark 1824 case of *Gibbons v. Ogden*, navigation along an interstate waterway is considered interstate commerce even if the journey takes place solely within a single state.[15] Essentially, what *Wabash* did was to extend that reasoning to rail transport.

Wabash likely hastened the passage of the Interstate Commerce Act a year later.[16] The act required that railroad rates be reasonable, just, and public; prohibited short-haul/long-haul rate discrimination; and established the first independent federal regulatory agency, the Interstate Commerce Commission (ICC), to oversee and enforce the act. It did not give the ICC the power to fix rates, although later legislation did.[17]

Subsequent laws—some referred to by Worthy Master Newsom—gave the ICC authority over motor vehicles, air transport, and water carriers. In *Federal Power Commission v. Hope Natural Gas,* the Supreme Court established a policy of evaluating the end result of a rate-making decision in balancing the competing interests of consumers and investors instead of analyzing rate-making methodology.[18]

What began with the Granger cases thus grew into an elaborate regulatory system that governed most modern methods of transportation for many years. Ascertaining what was best for the public was the guiding principle. During the 1970s and 1980s, interpretation of what seems good for public welfare shifted and substantial deregulation occurred, beginning with the Railroad Revitalization and Regulatory Reform Act (1976) and followed by the Airline Deregulation Act (1978), the Staggers Rail Act (1980), and the Motor Carrier Act (1980). This in turn has led to more questions about the role of regulatory agencies in promoting public well-being.[19]

Chapter 2 also mentioned the Minnesota Rate Cases, headlined by *Chicago, Milwaukee, and St. Paul Railway Company v. Minnesota.* Here, a Minnesota law made the railroad commission the final judge of the reasonableness of railroad rates. The Supreme Court determined that this law violated the due process clause of the Fourteenth Amendment. The court decided that parties should instead have judicial review available as an option. Judicial review of legislation was an established doctrine in American law under *Marbury v. Madison,* but it took the Minnesota Rate Cases to extend the doctrine to regulation. These cases, which grew directly out of the Granger cases, gave rise to an ongoing discussion in many areas of the law about how the legislative and judicial branches should interact.[20]

Other Law

The Granger laws generated later cases and statutes concerning mass transit, but they also raised questions about what could be regulated, by whom, and how. Some scholars think the Grange and the laws they inspired indirectly led to the passage of the Sherman Act (1890) and other antitrust laws.[21] Numerous lawsuits contemplate what constitutes interstate commerce and what "clothed with a public interest" could mean. What follows is by no means a complete list of cases, but it gives a flavor of the breadth of issues generated by the Granger laws.

Several cases in the 1920s tackled the question of interstate commerce. Were stockyards engaged in interstate commerce? The court in *Stafford v. Wallace, Burton v. Clyne* said yes: "Stockyards are but a throat through which the current [of livestock] flows, and the transactions which occur therein are only incident to this current from . . . one State to another." How about the Chicago Board of Trade when it dealt in grain futures? Once again, the answer was yes: the US Supreme Court determined in *Board of Trade v. Olsen* that the board "conducts a business which is affected with a public interest."[22]

But the court would not consider a meat-packing company in the same light. Here the question was whether a wage floor conflicted with the Fourteenth Amendment. The court in *Charles Wolff Packing Company v. Court of Industrial Relations of Kansas* said it did and ruled that a statute requiring a minimum wage interfered with freedom of contract and was unconstitutional.[23] The *Wolff* court distinguished the company from a "common carrier which accepts a railroad franchise." A common carrier "is not free to withdraw the use of that which it has granted to the public. . . . It may give up its franchise and enterprise, but short of this, it must continue. . . . The minutely detailed government supervision, including that of their relations to their employees, to which the railroads of the country have been gradually subjected by Congress through its power over interstate commerce, furnishes no precedent for regulation of the business . . . whose classification as public is at the best doubtful."

Minimum-wage and maximum-hours legislation found it difficult at first to pass the "public interest" test, despite an argument made by the Minnesota attorney general in 1897 that commissions resembling those for railroads could carry out these labor-market provisions. A minimum wage law for females in private employment was deemed an unconstitutional interference with the freedom to contract and an invalid exercise of state police power, according to

Legacies of the Grange

the 1923 case of *Adkins et al. v. Children's Hospital*. Although the court thought restricting miners' hours was in the public interest in *Holden v. Hardy*, heard in 1898, it decided seven years later in *Lochner v. New York*, that maximum hours' legislation for bakers was not, because baking was not inherently dangerous. Justice Oliver Wendell Holmes Jr. dissented in *Lochner*, saying, "A constitution is not intended to embody a particular economic theory, whether of paternalism and the organic relation of the citizen to the State or of laissez faire. It is made for people of fundamentally differing views, and the accident of our finding certain opinions natural and familiar or novel and even shocking ought not to conclude our judgment upon the question whether statutes embodying them conflict with the Constitution of the United States."[24]

One notable counter to *Lochner* was the 1908 case of *Muller v. Oregon*. The difference here was the sex of the worker. In *Muller*, the court determined that restricting women working in laundries to a ten-hour workday was reasonable, because "the physical well-being of woman becomes an object of public interest and care in order to preserve the strength and vigor of the race."[25]

The case of *Berea College v. Kentucky*, heard the same year as *Muller*, offers a different sort of contrast to *Lochner*. Here, the court essentially repudiated its own arguments in *Lochner* about freedom of contract by upholding a Kentucky law that prohibited Berea, a private institution, from operating on an integrated basis. As one noted scholar argues, the *Berea* decision is completely inconsistent with *Lochner* and displays the racial bias of the Supreme Court at this time.[26]

Although laws about minimum wage and maximum hours did not yet generally have the court's full blessing as meeting a "public interest" test, a DC statute allowing tenants to remain in the property past the term of the lease passed muster as long as rent payments continued. The court in *Block v. Hirsh* said that such statutes were passed for public health reasons to address severe housing limitations due to increased residency in the capital city during World War I.[27] The opinion found the law reasonable because it was limited in time and allowed landlords to receive "reasonable" rent. Given the housing shortage, however, what was reasonable to the court might differ substantially from free-market rental rates. Landlords certainly had an argument that they were forgoing substantial rent premiums because of the law.

Price and wage regulation—like railroad rate regulation in the Grange cases—eventually became viewed as a matter of public interest and a legitimate exercise of police power. In the 1934 case of *Nebbia v. New York,* the court upheld a New York statute regulating the wholesale and retail prices of milk; a storekeeper who sold milk at a discount was convicted and fined. In contrast to *Adkins,* the 1937 case of *West Coast Hotel v. Parrish* supported the principle of minimum wage laws for women, with the opinion stating, "What can be closer to the public interest than the health of women and their protection from unscrupulous and overreaching employers?" It therefore decided that the Washington statute prescribing a wage floor for females met the due process test laid out in the Fourteenth Amendment.[28]

U.S. v. Carolene Products upheld the constitutionality of a 1923 Congressional Act forbidding the interstate shipment of "filled milk" (milk with vegetable oil added).[29] This case, like *Nebbia* and *West Coast Hotel,* deferred to legislative judgment about public health matters and essentially gave the green light to most forms of economic regulation. *Carolene* is perhaps more famous, however, for a footnote that advocated greater scrutiny of statutes directed at minorities. Although the court did not immediately adopt this view, the footnote foreshadowed what would take place some thirty years later.

The Granger cases thus gave rise to questions about procedure as well as substance. In particular, what was the role of the courts vis-à-vis legislative and regulatory bodies? *Munn* required the court to presume that statutes were constitutional. The majority applied this presumption in one of the best-known cases of the late nineteenth century: *Plessy v. Ferguson. Plessy* upheld the right of states to maintain racial segregation on trains and served as a cornerstone in the effort to segregate blacks from whites in the United States for decades. The sole dissent in *Plessy* came from Justice John Marshall Harlan, who acknowledged that the state had a well-established right to regulate railroads but objected to the arbitrary separation of citizens on the basis of race, calling it a badge of servitude inconsistent with the Thirteenth, Fourteenth, and Fifteenth Amendments. As Harlan presciently put it, "In my opinion, the judgment this day rendered will, in time, prove to be quite as pernicious as the decision made by this tribunal in the *Dred Scott* case."[30]

Despite the *Carolene* footnote, the court's hands-off approach lasted through the 1960s in many sorts of cases. Justice Hugo Black in the 1963 case of *Ferguson v. Skrupa* warned that the US Supreme Court should not act as a superlegislature, for instance.[31] He supported the legislature's right to enact anything having to do with social conditions as long as it was reasonable and had some relation to the legislature's purpose.

But the court's deference to legislative mandates had already begun to wane by the time *Ferguson* was heard, particularly in segregation cases. Justice William O. Douglas concurred with the opinion in *Garner v. Louisiana* in throwing out convictions for disturbing the peace by black defendants (represented by counsels Jack Greenberg and Thurgood Marshall) who sat at a white lunch counter. As Justice Douglas put it, "Restaurants are a part of the public life," and "though they are private enterprises, they are public facilities in which the States may not enforce a policy of racial segregation."[32]

Justice Black found himself on the losing side in the landmark 1965 case of *Griswold v. Connecticut;* Black appealed to *Munn* in his dissent. In *Griswold,* a doctor and a director of a medical clinic were convicted of violating a state law that prohibited the dispensing of birth control devices to married couples. The court found legitimate the right of privacy to use birth control, and Justices John Marshall Harlan II (grandson of the justice in *Plessy*) and Byron White relied on the due process clause of the Fourteenth Amendment to call the statute unconstitutional. Justice Black responded that *Munn* required the court to presume statutes were constitutional and stated that the court should "exercise restraint" in determining unconstitutionality. In Black's view, the majority under Justice Douglas violated the *Munn* presumption and now required statutes to bear a "substantial burden of justification when attacked under the Fourteenth Amendment."[33]

The court's use of the reasoning in *Munn* has frustrated environmentalists, however. The court adhered to the position held in *Ferguson* in a key 1978 case: *Duke Power v. Carolina Environmental Study Group, Inc.* Here, the court decided that Congress had not acted in an arbitrary or irrational manner in enacting a statute that limited the liability of the nuclear power industry and thus refused to call the statute unconstitutional because it did not violate the due process clause of the Fifth Amendment. Both the Fifth and the Fourteenth Amendments contain a due process clause; the only difference is that the Fourteenth Amendment specifies that no state shall deprive any person of life, liberty, or property without due process of law whereas the Fifth Amendment simply says that no person shall be deprived of life, liberty, or property without due process of law. Today's Supreme Court effectively applies the two due process clauses in the same manner.[34] Plaintiffs in *Duke* included environmental organizations and people who lived near the power plant.

Environmentalists took another blow in the important 1992 case of *Lucas v. South Carolina Coastal Council.* In *Lucas,* the plaintiff bought two lots on which he intended to build houses. The state then enacted the Beachfront Management Act, which barred him from erecting any permanent habitable structures on his land. Although the South Carolina Supreme Court denied the landowner compensation under the takings clauses of the Fifth and Fourteenth Amendments, the US Supreme Court reversed and remanded the case because it considered relevant the regulation's effect on the property value. Justice John Paul Stevens dissented, quoting *Munn:* "The Court's holding today effectively freezes the State's common law, denying the legislature much of its traditional power to revise the law governing the rights and uses of property. Until today, I had thought we had long ago abandoned this approach to constitutional law. More than a century ago we recognized that 'the great office of statutes is to remedy defects in the common law as they are developed, and to adapt it to the changes of time and circumstances.'"[35]

The court's acerbic reaction to recent constitutional challenges to the Patient Protection and Affordable Care Act in *National Federation of Independent Business, et al., v. Sebelius* (and related cases) supports Justice Black's position that it should not sit as a superlegislature. The opinion states the court's "general reticence to invalidate the acts of the Nation's elected leaders. . . . Members of this Court are vested with the authority to interpret the law; we possess neither the expertise nor the prerogative to make policy judgments. Those decisions are entrusted to our Nation's elected leaders, who can be thrown out of office if the people disagree with them. It is not our job to protect the people from the consequences of their political choices."[36]

Some recent cases that thrash out what roles the judiciary and the legislature should play in crafting law have an added layer: federalism. *Lucas,* mentioned above, is one. Another is *Bush v. Gore,* in which the US Supreme Court effectively stepped in to overturn the Florida Supreme Court's interpretation of Florida statutes involving recounted ballots.[37] Opinions were split—nearly in half—at both the state and the federal levels.

The two momentous decisions of the US Supreme Court's 2013 term—*U.S. v. Windsor* and *Shelby County v. Holder*—also demonstrate the ongoing strong opinions on both sides concerning just what sort of power the judiciary has in nullifying legislation. In the first, the court struck down a portion of the 1996 Defense of Marriage Act which denied federal benefits to same-sex couples who were legally married. In the second, the court deemed unconstitutional a section of the 1965 Voting Rights Act that had required certain states and localities to obtain clearance from federal authorities before changing voting laws or practices. Although these cases are only tangentially related to the Granger cases in any legal sense, they nevertheless show that the questions the Granger cases raised about what could be regulated, how, and by whom are still pertinent today.[38]

Concluding Thoughts

Dismissing the Grange movement as a short-lived nineteenth-century farmer uprising against railroads and middlemen is tempting. After all, its decline was as abrupt and massive as its initial growth, even though a remnant of the organization lives on.

But writing off the Patrons of Husbandry as a flash in the pan would be a mistake. They created a template for all subsequent American agricultural organizations and supplied inspiration for other types of groups as well. They provide a key historical example of how cooperative economic endeavors can succeed—and why they fail. The Grange also occupies a vital position in American legal history, because legislation associated with it raised critical issues about the role of the state in regulating private industry as well as the interactions of legislatures and courts. And the minutes from the Minnehaha subordinate allow us to peer into the workings of a long-lived American voluntary communal association to understand better how it served the economic, social, educational, and cultural needs of its members throughout the century of its existence.

Perhaps most important, the Grangers as a group constituted one of the first and strongest voices questioning the hazards of extreme wealth inequality for a society. Although they may enjoy more credit than is due for the "Granger laws" that instituted railroad regulation in this country, many Grangers were certainly on the side of those who fought for such laws. The questions raised there about the nature and governance of public goods remain salient. I suspect the founders of the Grange would be pleased to know this, for they enshrined in their *Declaration of Purposes* this belief: "We acknowledge the broad principle that difference of opinion is no crime, and hold that progress toward truth is made by differences of opinion."

Notes

Introduction

1. Wright [1874] 1885.
2. Approval for the Carrabelle and Thomasville appears in Florida 1881, Chapter 3339 [No. 121], 161–62. Railroad mileage is reported in Carter et al. (2006), Series Df884.
3. 94 U.S. 113 (1877).
4. Tontz (1964); Dyson (1986); and Rothstein (1988) offer details about other agricultural associations.
5. Public Law 111–48.

Chapter 1: "Our Agricultural Brotherhood"

1. General Kirby Smith surrendered the last major Confederate forces on 26 May 1865, although President Johnson did not formally proclaim an end to the war until more than a year later (Long 1985). Kelley's trip is described in Buck ([1913] 1963, 41); Barns (1967, 229); and Woods (1991, 88).
2. Woods (1991, 99) details the early Grange activity. Farmers' clubs existed from the beginning of the republic. Dyson (1986, 99) states that at least 621 clubs were active in 20 states by the late 1850s; Calvert (1977, 182) says in 1860 a total of 941 farm societies existed in the United States. A loose collection of agricultural societies applied for the funds left by James Smithson in an attempt to create a national group. They were disappointed when Congress established the Smithsonian Institution instead (Dyson 1986, 1–2). Another long-lived farm organization is the American Pomological Society, which formed in 1849 and had 900 members in 1984 (Dyson 1986, 138).
3. The long-accepted figure of 650,000 deaths among Union and Confederate soldiers has recently been revised upward to 752,000 (Hacker 2011). These numbers do not include civilian deaths. The US population in 1860 was 31,443,321, which included 3.95 million slaves (Carter et al., Series Aa145, Aa148). Franklin (1970, 381) reports on the Mississippi state budget; Buck ([1913] 1963, 25–28) and Dyson (1986, 233–34) describe the plight of the farmers. Ketcham (2014) offers details about Wilder's experiences.
4. J. Smith (2001).
5. Bourne (2010, 2013).
6. Soltow (1975); Rosenbloom and Stutes (2005).

7. Opinions of Kelley's farming abilities vary. Woods (1991, chap. 2) paints a fairly sympathetic view, casting Kelley as an innovative experimenter who pioneered the collection and use of statistics as a means of improving yields. Grange scholar Solon Buck ([1913] 1963, 41–42) views Kelley as the father of the Patrons of Husbandry, although Barns (1967, 235–37) suggests that the contributions of cofounder William Saunders may be underappreciated. Gilman and Smith (1967, 331) refer to Kelley's membership in the St. Paul Masonic lodge.

8. Woods (1991, 23, 27, 51–56) gives details about Kelley's personal history; Bourne (2011) analyzes railroad stock prices.

9. Barns (1967, 230) tells of Kelley's move to Washington, and Buck ([1913] 1963, 41–42) describes his fellow Grange organizers.

10. Tontz (1964, Table 1); Wicker (2000). Because farm population has been shrinking since about 1910 (except for a brief increase in the 1930s), the percentage of farmers belonging to the Grange actually grew slightly over the twentieth century, up to about 5 percent in 1960 (Tontz 1964, Table 1; Carter et al. 2006, series Da14).

11. National Grange (2012), Bylaw 4.3.5 (B).

12. Woods (1991, 100); Dyson (1986, 236); and *Chicago Inter Ocean* (13 November 1886) describe the shaky beginning.

13. D. Johnston (1904, 258) and Dyson (1986, 235) talk about general early efforts, and Calvert (1977, 183–85) relates A. J. Rose's experiences in Texas.

14. The all-time Minnesota record is held by William B. Pearson, State Worthy Master for several years, who organized 137 subordinates between 1932 and 1962.

15. Details appear in Buck ([1913] 1963, 66–67); Tontz (1964, 148); Dyson (1986, 236); Rothstein (1988, 169); Ferry (2004); *Philadelphia Evening Bulletin* (21 July 1874); and Minnesota State Grange records (box 2). Indiana now has 1008 townships in 92 counties.

16. Minnesota State Grange records, box 2.

17. National Grange (2012), Bylaws 4.3.3 (A), 4.6.10; Woods (1991, 95). The National Grange is now a delegate body composed of senior-status Grangers.

18. Woods (1991, 166–67).

19. The Grange was not the first to extend "equal" membership to women—that honor belongs to the Independent Order of Good Templars, which was the only antebellum temperance movement to survive the war (Marti 1984, 248).

20. Marti (1984, 249). The Grange finally acknowledged Miss Hall as an equal founder in 1892 (Dyson 1986, 234).

21. Minnehaha Grange records, boxes 1 and 2; Minnesota State Grange records, box 2.

22. Marti (1984, 251–52). Ole Rolvaag's magnum opus, *Giants in the Earth* (1927), tells of the loneliness, depression, and eventual insanity suffered by Norwegian immigrant women living in the desolate Dakota Territory.

23. Minnehaha Grange records, box 1. Dues information and descriptions of the female role appear in Buck ([1913] 1963, 48); Woods (1991, 168–69); and Keillor (2000, 37).

24. Partin (1957, 50). Woods (1991, 90) also refers to the Masonic influence.

25. *Ready Reference* (1914). Box 2 of the Minnehaha Grange records contains a Fuller pamphlet.

26. Prices appear in *Catalog* (1928) and Minnehaha Grange records, box 2. Conversion factors to today's prices are calculated from Carter et al. (2006), Series Cc2 and http://www.bls.gov.org/cpi/.

27. National Grange (2012), Bylaw 4.3.5 (C). Buck ([1913] 1963, 43) and Woods (1991, 99, chap. 10) describe the degrees.

28. National Grange (2012).

29. Entries are from 20 October 1956, 4 March 1961, and 3 March 1962.

30. Barns (1967, 242).

31. Walker (1893, 69–72).

32. Coase (1960) and Olson (1965) discuss transactions costs and collective action.

33. Ransom and Sutch (1977).

34. Woods (1991, 43).

35. http://www.cprr.org/Museum/RR_Development.html#3; Detrick (1903, 250); Carter et al. (2006), series Df884.

36. For details, see Hart (1887); Walker (1893, 74); Buck ([1913] 1963, 12, 23–24, 53); Crawford (1939, 253–55); Miles (1967b, 10–11); Miller (1971); Dyson (1986, 234); Woods (1991, 81); and Kanazawa and Noll (1994, 19–20).

37. Saloutos (1948, 167); Fogel (1964); and Fishlow (1965) feature discussions of the effects of railroad expansion.

38. Woods (1991, 141).

39. Smalley (1906, 5–8).

40. Saloutos (1953, 482–83). However, most "redeemer" constitutions—in Texas, Arkansas, and Louisiana, for example—did include clauses denoting railroads as "common carriers" so they could reserve the power to regulate them at some point (Calvert 1977, 185). Examples of railroad studies are McAfee (1968, 52); Miller (1971, 663); and Kanazawa and Noll (1994, 15).

41. Paul (1958, 332).

42. Correlation coefficients indicate the statistical relationship between two variables and range from -1 to +1. A value of -1 shows the variables are perfectly negatively correlated whereas a value of +1 indicates perfect positive correlation. This coefficient of 0.67 implies a strong positive relationship between the two variables.

43. The number of subordinates per thousand of population was on average 0.244 in counties with no railroads, 0.711 in counties with one railroad, and 0.559 in counties with multiple railroads. Over 70 percent of populated counties with no railroads also had no subordinates; of populated counties with railroads, fewer than 20 percent had no subordinates.

44. Schell (1936, 63).
45. Mixon (2008).
46. 149 U.S. 304 (1893). Buck ([1913] 1963, 21); Crawford (1939, 271–72); Saloutos (1948, 168); and Miles (1967b, 10) discuss tax structure.
47. Carter et al. (2006), Series Ca11; Sutch (2006).
48. Buck ([1913] 1963, 52); Calvert (1977, 181).
49. Saloutos (1953, 475–78); Dyson (1986, 47–49); and Baum and Calvert (1989, 37).
50. Entries are from 6 March 1954 and 1 June 1957.
51. *Philadelphia Evening Bulletin* (12 January 1874).
52. Baum and Calvert (1989, 49) relate the Texas episode, and Crawford (1939, 245) reports the Washington Grangers' actions.
53. Buck ([1913] 1963, 34).

Chapter 2: The Granger Railroad Laws

1. The Grangers proudly continue to use the term "Granger laws." For example, at the one hundredth meeting of the National Grange in November 1966 in Minneapolis, Worthy Master Herschel Newsom referred to the "famous Granger Laws" and praised the organization for its contributions to national transportation policy.
2. Miles (1967a, 24) considers the Granger laws as providing much-needed protection to the people, for example, but Supreme Court Justice Stephen Field indicates his dismay with what he perceives as interference with private property in his *Munn* dissent, discussed later in the chapter.
3. At some point, however, my use of the streetlight could cast a shadow, which then could affect the benefit you receive from it. Arthur Pigou's ([1920] 1932) classic example of a public good is a lighthouse. Coase (1974) refutes this example, because British lighthouses were sometimes privately owned. Countering Coase is Van Zandt (1993).
4. See, for example, Coates and Humphreys (2008).
5. Miller (1971); Boden (1971, 252).
6. 17 U.S. 518 (1819). The contract clause appears in Art. 1, §9.
7. 11 Peters 420 (1837).
8. Levy (1957) and Kutler (1971) analyze the *Charles River Bridge* case.
9. None of the bills succeeded. Even earlier, New York and Pennsylvania initially required railroads that were competing with canals to contribute to the costs of canal maintenance. Other mid-Atlantic states imposed transit taxes on interstate shipments until courts declared this an interference with interstate commerce; some states then refused to allow out-of-state companies to build lines within the state. These early experiences alerted the public—and the Grangers—to the influence of railroads in shaping state policy (Merk 1949). New York State levied a special tax on freight carried by railroads that competed with state-owned canals. And states charged higher tolls on goods produced out of state than those from in state for travel on state-owned canals

(Scheiber 1971, 1035). According to Scheiber (1971, 1037), several riparian and admiralty cases included the language "affected with a public interest" long before Justice Matthew Hale used the phrase in the Granger cases.

10. Klement (1952, 692; 1960).

11. The article appeared on 23 February 1874. Buck ([1913] 1963, 96); Klement (1952, 679); and Miller (1971) discuss the legislation in the various states.

12. Buck ([1913] 1963, 126, 129–30); Klement (1952, 692); Kanazawa and Noll (1994, 15, 33).

13. Buck ([1913] 1963, 159, 162); Ridge (1956, 704–5); Naftalin (1956, 56); Woods (1991, 156).

14. Buck ([1913] 1963, 166).

15. Buck ([1913] 1963, 181).

16. 94 U.S. 113 (1877). The other cases—which did concern railroads—include *Chicago Burlington and Quincy Railroad v. Iowa,* 94 U.S. 155; *Peik v. Chicago and Northwestern Railroad* (and *Lawrence v. same*), 94 U.S. 164; *Chicago, Milwaukee, and St. Paul Railroad v. Ackley,* 94 U.S. 179; *Winona & St. Peter Railroad Company v. Blake,* 94 U.S. 180; and *Stone v. Wisconsin,* 94 U.S. 181. Some commentators use the erroneous date of 1876 for these cases, due to a mistake by Supreme Court Reporter William Otto (Sigmund 1953). Some scholars include additional cases or subtract from this list, but most enumerate the cases above as the "Granger cases."

17. Buck ([1913] 1963, 207–8).

18. 94 U.S. 181, 183 (1877).

19. Miller (1954); Woodman (1962); Treleven (1969); Rothstein (1988, 168–69).

20. Treleven (1969).

21. Miller (1954).

22. Woodman (1962, 19, 24).

23. Anfinson (2003, 83). The Chicago and Rock Island line crossed the river in 1856; the panic of 1857 and the Civil War put a lid on construction for a time. But three more railroads went across the river between 1866 and 1869, and by 1877 thirteen railroad bridges spanned the upper Mississippi (Anfinson 2003, 80).

24. Anfinson (2003, 83, 85); *Baltimore Sun* (23 February 1874).

25. 22 U.S. 1 (1824).

26. www.usace.army.mil.

27. Annual population growth was just over 4 percent between 1860 and 1870 in Missouri, and just over 2 percent between 1870 and 1880. By comparison, annual US population growth in those two periods was just over 2 percent over the entire period (Carter et al. 2006, Series Aa7, Aa3583, Aa4404). Kansas was relatively unsettled in 1860, in part due to uncertainty about its status regarding slavery. After it entered the Union as a free state in January 1861 and the Homestead Act was passed in 1862, settlers began arriving in greater numbers.

28. *Philadelphia Inquirer* (21 July 1874).

29. Gustin (1875, 59, 60, 72).
30. Buck ([1913] 1963, 149); Naftalin (1956, 55); Miller (1971).
31. *Philadelphia Evening Bulletin* (13 July 1874).
32. Detrick (1903); Buck ([1913] 1963, 23).
33. *Chicago Inter Ocean* (3 March 1877).
34. Johnson (1908).
35. 118 U.S. 557 (1886), 49 U.S.C. §101 et seq.
36. 134 U.S. 418 (1890).

Chapter 3: The Grange's Ambitious Experiments with Private Cooperation

1. Barns (1967, 241); Dyson (1986, 236–37); Keillor (2000, 41).
2. *New Orleans Daily Picayune* (13 July 1873).
3. The classic treatise on game theory is von Neumann and Morgenstern (1944).
4. Foster (1894, 109); Buck ([1913] 1963, 240, 270); Dyson (1986, 58); Keillor (2000, 65).
5. Paul (1958, 334).
6. Donnelly (1873).
7. Minnehaha Grange records (box 2).
8. Schell (1936, 80).
9. Buck ([1913] 1963, 45); Keillor (2000, 41).
10. *Baltimore Sun* (12 February 1874); Cerny (1963, 188); *Georgia Weekly Telegraph* (Macon, GA, 19 August 1873).
11. Hull (1937, 108).
12. Keillor (2000, 6).
13. Ferguson (1942, 511).
14. *Georgia Weekly Telegraph* (Macon, GA, 17 February 1874); Buck ([1913] 1963, 243); Vale (1966); Dyson (1986, 237–38); Woods (1991, 162).
15. Entries are from 17 November 1883, 3 May 1884, 5 July 1884, 4 April 1909, 15 April 1910, 18 April 1902, 20 May 1911, 16 December 1911, and 20 January 1917.
16. Entries are from 6 June 1879 and 20 April 1875.
17. Saloutos (1953, 487).
18. R. Smith (1939); Calvert (1977, 194); Davis (1945); Ferguson (1942).
19. http://www.grange.org/texasstate/; http://www.nationalgrange.org.
20. *Wheeling Daily Register* (27 December 1878); Rothstein (1988, 169); Schell (1936).
21. R. Smith (1939, 300); Saloutos (1953, 487); Partin (1957, 59); Dyson (1986, 58).
22. Calvert (1977, 191, 190) and Rothstein (1988, 169) discuss the failures of southern co-ops.
23. Foster (1894, 106, 109); Buck ([1913] 1963, 260); Schell (1936, 72); Hull (1937).
24. Cerny (1963, 204).

25. Buck ([1913] 1963, 243, 267); Saloutos (1948, 172); Keillor (2000, 72).
26. *Philadelphia Evening Bulletin* (29 July 1874); Buck ([1913] 1963, 257).
27. Davis (1945, 349–50).
28. Buck ([1913] 1963, 247); Paul (1958, 348–49).
29. Hirsch (1929, 496). Saloutos (1953, 481) refers to the Liverpool agent problem.
30. Foster (1894, 104); Keillor (2000, 77); Buck ([1913] 1963, 257); Woods (1991, 192).
31. Buck ([1913] 1963, 68); Dyson (1986, 240); Woods (1991, 196).
32. Partin (1957, 58); Minnehaha Grange records (boxes 1 and 2).
33. Dyson (1986, 19–23, 214–32, 286); Rothstein (1988, appendix).
34. Woods (1991, 205).
35. *Baltimore Sun* (2 June 1874). Ander (1934, 161, 168) reports on church grievances; Schell (1936, 75) and Keillor (2000, 38) tell of the Minnesota immigrant Granges. According to Rothstein (1988, 177) one of the most successful farmers' movements in the twentieth century was the North Dakota Non Partisan League, apparently open to all. Lutherans and Catholics joined together to establish a state-owned grain elevator, flour mills, banks, and insurance firm. When this organization opposed the draft during World War I, its members switched allegiance to the Farm Bureau.
36. Baum and Calvert (1989, 43).
37. Foster (1894, 109); Rothstein (1988, 169); http://www.nationalgrange.org.
38. Prescott (1970); Rothstein (1988, 177). Another recent movement is community-sponsored agriculture (CSA), where consumers pledge to support local farms. CSA started in the United States in the 1980s and has enjoyed some popularity but is not particularly lucrative for farmers.
39. http://milkinggotmilk.com/campaign-history/.
40. 7 U.S.C. 2901–11, 544 U.S. 550 (2005).
41. http://abcnews.go.com/blogs/politics/2011/11/obama-administration-to-delay-new-15-cent-christmas-tree-fee/.
42. Ridge (1956, 700, 709); Tontz (1964, 149); Garwood (1968, 178); McMath (1975, xi); Dyson (1986, 189, 192, 239); Field (1998, 22).
43. Schwantes (1985, 10); Dyson (1986, 293–94).
44. Dyson (1986, 188, 190, 197–98, 200).
45. Dyson (1986, 14).
46. http://www.azcentral.com/12news/news/articles/20120328feds-cesar-chavez-life-historic-status-key-sites.html; http://www.sisepuedefilm.com/pages/story.html.
47. *Morning Oregonian* (Portland, OR, 11 May 1910). Dyson (1986, 15–19) discusses the Farm Bureau, and Buck ([1913] 1963, 62) refers to charter revocation by the Grange.
48. Prescott (1977).
49. Pub. Law 37–108, 7 U.S.C. §361a et seq.

50. Kile (1948); Tontz (1964, 150).

51. A joint meeting occurred on 17 October 1931, for example. This Grange also worked closely with the local American Legion, particularly in putting together Memorial Day celebrations (18 April 1953, 15 May 1954, and 5 April 1958). Dyson (1986, 249) reports the united appeal to President Hoover.

52. *Grand Rapids (MI) Herald* (21 April 1900); *Aberdeen (SD) Weekly* (22 June 1911); *Philadelphia Inquirer* (26 November 1911). For details on the financial panics, see Wicker (2000).

53. Minnesota State Grange records (box 2).

54. http://www.linkedin.com/company/national-grange. Dyson (1986, 252) refers to the confidentiality issue.

55. Buck ([1913] 1963, 270); Saloutos (1948, 172); Keillor (2000, 51).

56. Entries are from 9 April 1921 and 7 January 1956.

57. http://www.grange.com/.

58. http://www.insurance.ohio.gov/Company/MC/2009/GrangeMutual.pdf.

59. Entries are from 4 February 1950, 15 May 1954, 19 March 1955, and 7 September 1957.

60. http://www.snopud.com/?p=1349; http://www.keepthelightsonoregon.org/history.html; "Energy Adviser" (2012). Many thanks to Mike Kleiner for educating me about public utility districts in the Pacific Northwest.

61. Minnehaha Grange records (box 2).

62. http://www.minnpost.com/two-cities/2013/08/minneapolis-utility-takeover-unions-and-businesses-join-forces-against-energy-act; http://minnesota.publicradio.org/display/web/2013/08/09/environment/xcel-minneapolis-agree-on-green-energy-goals.

Chapter 4: The Grange as a Fraternal, Educational, and Charitable Organization

1. Hartman (2013).

2. *Philadelphia Inquirer* (28 August 1875); Buck ([1913] 1963, 61); Dyson (1986, 242, 248, 250).

3. Minnesota State Grange records (boxes 2 and 3).

4. Black's Bend Grange in Alabama tried meeting twice a month, then went down to once, and finally dissolved (Partin 1957, 52).

5. T. Martin (2009). Average January temperature in Minneapolis is 11.8° F (http://www.climate-zone.com/climate/united-states/minnesota/minneapolis-stpaul/).

6. https://www.facebook.com/pages/Minnesota-State-Grange/114337321976493.

7. Entries include 19 March 1938, 7 November 1942, 21 November 1942, 21 April 1951, 19 April 1952, 21 March 1953, 18 April 1953, 5 June 1954, 4 September 1954, 21 May 1955, 17 November 1956, 2 March 1957, 20 April 1957, 7 January 1961, 1 April 1961, 3 June 1961, 7 October 1961, 21 October 1961, and 5 September 1964.

8. Entries are from 15 April 1939, 15 June 1940, 7 December 1940, 5 February 1949, 21 January 1950, 21 March 1953, 16 May 1953, 3 June 1953, 2 February 1957, and 16 May 1959.

9. Entries are from 6 February 1954 (referring to proceedings from the 1880s), 7 September 1968, 2 June 1972, and October 1975.

10. Entries are from 21 February 1874, 7 April 1888, 8 May 1909, 1 April 1911, 21 April 1917, 6 May 1918, 3 May 1919, 15 May 1920, and 18 June 1938.

11. Entry is from 21 April 1917.

12. Entries are from 5 September 1955 and 17 January 1958.

13. Entries are from 4 April 1909, 21 January 1911, 16 April 1949, and 7 March 1964.

14. Entries are from 2 December 1876, 7 April 1888, 20 November 1915, 8 May 1909, 16 March 1883, 4 May 1883, 30 November 1886, 21 November 1908, 6 May 1905, 1 April 1911, 29 August 1879, 4 February 1911, and 18 September 1938.

15. Entries are from 21 November 1908 and 6 November 1920.

16. Saloutos (1953, 485); Ferguson (1942, 500–501); Partin (1957, 55); Crawford (1939, 267); R. Smith (1939, 314–50).

17. Entries are from 4 January 1958, 1 April 1944, and 18 March 1888.

18. Ferguson (1942, 498–502); Saloutos (1953, 484–86).

19. Ferguson (1942, 505).

20. Marti (1982, 440).

21. The *Bellingham (WA) Herald* (29 September 1911) reports a similar concern by the Whatcom County Pomona, which was adamantly opposed to paying off the county's debts because there was "no check to prevent the county officers from going ahead and piling up more indebtedness."

22. http://www.nationalgrange.org.

23. Marti (1984, 253–54). Crawford (1939, 268), Ferguson (1942, 505–6, 512), and Partin (1957, 54) discuss public speaking and other skills acquired in various Granges.

24. Entries are from 1 February 1919, 6 January 1940, 18 May 1940, 5 April 1941, 19 April 1941, 3 April 1943, 5 June 1948, 1 November 1952, 4 April 1959, and 20 March 1954. Marti (1984, 254) also refers to discussions about home and gardening skills.

25. Entries are from 1 April 1905, 15 October 1938, 3 December 1938, 5 September 1942, 16 February 1952, 4 October 1952, 5 June 1965, 16 December 1922, 20 January 1923, 5 March 1938, and 7 March 1964.

26. Entries are from 3 June 1950, 6 November 1943, 4 October 1958, 4 June 1887.

27. Entries are from 16 March 1940, 7 January 1961, 6 October 1972, 17 April 1943, 6 December 1947, 20 May 1961, 4 January 1964, and 7 October 1944. Fire safety was also a topic at the 1957 Corn States Grange Lecturer Conference (Minnehaha Grange, box 2).

28. Entries are from 15 October 1960, 2 September 1961, 5 May 1961, 2 December 1961, 17 November 1962, 3 October 1948, 6 October 1956, and 5 May 1962.

29. Entries are from 4 October 1947, 19 January 1952, 19 March 1938, 16 March 1946, 22 May 1947, and 19 February 1949. Elsewhere, Mississippi Granges even started libraries and newspapers (Ferguson 1942, 507).

30. http://www.nationalgrange.org/our-values/develop-character-leadership/.

31. Entries are from 18 April 1902, 6 May 1905, 19 March 1949, 17 January 1953, 7 April 1956, 7 June 1957, 18 November 1961, 2 April 1966, and 4 June 1966.

32. Marti (1984, 255–58).

33. Wisc. Stat. 97.18, Dupré (1999). California has now surpassed Wisconsin in milk production.

34. Shipstead was a member of the Farmer-Labor Party at the time but switched to the Republicans in 1941. Schall was originally a Progressive but had turned to the Republicans by 1933. Legally blind, Schall is one of the few US Senators to have died in a road accident while in office—he was struck and killed by a hit-and-run driver in Maryland in 1935.

35. Concern about alcohol permeates Grange records. In Texas, for example, Grangers and former Grangers united to try to amend the state constitution in 1887 to prohibit alcohol (Baum and Calvert 1989, 53–54). The *Wilkes-Barre Times Leader* (25 February 1916) tells of Pomona Grange no. 31 of Montour and Northumberland counties going on record against the rum traffic and advocating nationwide prohibition. This Grange also favored federal control of telephone and telegraph lines.

36. http://www.nationalgrange.org.

37. http://www.wa-grange.org/, http://www.californiagrange.org/, http://www.sonomacountygazette.com/cms/pages/sonoma-county-news-article-3219.html, http://www.pagrange.org/, http://www.nysgrange.org/, http://www.michiganstategrange.org/; http://www.nhgrange.org/Annual%20Convention/Info/2013%20Journal.pdf.

38. Entries are from 28 March 1874 and 17 September 1904.

39. Entries are from 20 February 1943, 1 December 1951, 2 February 1952, 21 November 1942, 15 May 1943, 17 May 1941, 20 September 1941, 7 February 1942, 19 September 1942, 15 May 1943, 2 September–7 October 1944, 1 April 1944, 18 February 1945, and 19 September 1942. Minnehaha Grangers had looked out for veterans of the first World War as well, providing them care packages when they were overseas and entertainment when they returned home (entries from 19 May 1918 and 18 January 1919).

40. Entries are from 21 March 1953, 6 November 1954, 18 February 1956, 5 April 1958, 7 December 1946, 19 March 1955, and 7 June 1958.

41. Entries are from 7 November 1953, 5 December 1953, 16 January 1954, 18 November 1961, 2 December 1961, 6 January 1962, and 1 February 1969.

42. Entries are from 4 September 1965, 21 January 1967, 1 March 1969, 7 June 1969, 6 September 1969, 19 September 1970, 7 April 1972, and 1 December 1973.

43. Entries are from 15 March 1952, 6 September 1952, 5 November 1955, 5 March 1971, 4 November 1967, 3 February 1968, 7 June 1969, 8 October 1971, 7 June 1969, 1 December 1973, 5 December 1959, 5 September 1964, 5 May 1978,

20 November 1948, 16 February 1952, 20 November 1954, 1 September 1962, 5 September 1964, 5 November 1966, and 4 November 1967.

44. Entries are from 20 November 1948, 3 June 1950, 7 February 1934, 3 January 1953, 20 February 1954, 16 November 1963, 7 June 1969, 8 September 1972, 1 December 1973, 7 April 1972, 5 December 1975, 3 April 1954, 1 March 1958, 7 November 1959, and 19 October 1963.

45. Entries are from 20 September 1941, 5 March 1960, 16 April 1960, 17 September 1960, 15 April 1961, 3 June 1953, 16 November 1946, 3 November 1951, 20 March 1954, and 19 February 1955.

46. http://www.massgrange.org/; http://www.illinoisgrange.org/.

47. Interview with T. J. Malaskee of the Kelley Grange.

48. For example, the Minnehaha held a sugaring off on 2 April 1887, a St. Patrick's Day dance party in March 1939, Christmas and New Year's Eve parties every year, Valentine parties (mentioned in 1946 and 1950), card parties (for instance on 18 May 1940, 19 January 1946, 7 April 1956, and 15 February 1964), potlucks (16 January 1942, 7 January 1972, 1 June 1973), singing (18 October 1952), caroling (5 December 1959), bingo (9 September 1950 and 5 November 1963), and bunco (17 November 1956 and 3 November 1962), among many other activities. These sorts of revelries also appear in the minutes of the Black's Bend Grange in Alabama (Partin 1957, 55–56).

49. Arthur et al. (1951, 5–6).

50. Putnam (2000).

Chapter 5: Legacies of the Grange

1. Davis (1945, 352); Buck ([1913] 1963, 279).

2. Buck ([1913] 1963, 310); Miles (1967a, 24).

3. Saloutos (1953, 487); Garwood (1968, 179); Calvert (1977, 182).

4. The Departments of Defense, Homeland Security, and Veterans Affairs have the largest number of employees, followed by Treasury, Justice, and Agriculture. (http://www.justice.gov/crt/508/report2/agencies.php). In terms of budget, Health and Human Services, Social Security, and Defense are the top spenders, followed by Agriculture (http://www.whitehouse.gov/omb/budget/Historicals, table 4.1).

5. Dyson (1986, 244); Dupré (1999).

6. Hirsch (1929, 493–94).

7. *Bellingham (WA) Herald* (8 April 1909).

8. Foster (1894, 109).

9. Naftalin (1956). Buck ([1913] 1963, 307) notes the analogy to the Knights of Labor; Naftalin (1956, 56) and Rothstein (1988, 170) discuss the other political parties.

10. Zuccotti Park in lower Manhattan was the first encampment for the Occupy movement, starting on 17 September 2011. It was dismantled two months later by New York police (http://www.nytimes.com/interactive/2011/10/05/nyregion/how-occupy-wall-street-turned-zuccotti-park-into-a-protest-camp.html; http://online.wsj.com/article/SB10001424052970204190504577039253668863814

.html). Susman and Tangel (2012) talk about the first anniversary of Occupy Wall Street, and Matthews (2012) refers to the spin-off groups.

11. Hale ([1670] 1787).
12. Falck (1967, 76); McCraw (1975).
13. A. Martin (1974); Kolko (1965); Stigler (1971).
14. Entry is from 14 November 1966.
15. 118 U.S. 557 (1886); Art. 1, §18, cl.3; 22 U.S. 1 (1824).
16. 49 U.S.C. §101 et seq. Some attribute the passage of the act in part to Milwaukee grain commission merchant Edward Bacon (Treleven 1969, 221). A. Martin (1974, 340) claims that New York City merchants bore more responsibility for the 1887 act than western farmers. He also suggests that the act was designed to assure customers of more stable rates (A. Martin 1974, 350–54).
17. Taylor (1936). This was only the start of railroad regulation. Next came the 1893 Railroad Safety Appliance Act, the 1901 act requiring the reporting of railroad accidents, the 1903 Elkins Act aiming at rebates, and the 1906 Hepburn Act increasing the size of the commission and giving it maximum-rate-making power. Although the case of *ICC v. Alabama Midland Railway*, 168 U.S. 144 (1897) gutted the short-haul/long-haul clause, the 1910 Mann-Elkins Act restored it.
18. Strand (1967); Kanazawa and Noll (1994, 22–23); 320 U.S. 591 (1944); Drobak (1985).
19. Rose-Ackerman (1990); Menard and Ghertman (2010).
20. 134 U.S. 418 (1890); 5 U.S. 137 (1803).
21. Arnold (1967).
22. 258 U.S. 495, 516 (1922); 262 U.S. 1, 40 (1923).
23. 262 U.S. 522, 543–44 (1923).
24. Miles (1967b); 261 U.S. 525 (1923); 169 U.S. 366 (1898); 198 U.S. 45, 54–55 (1905).
25. 208 U.S. 412 (1908).
26. 211 U.S. 45 (1908); Finkelman (2014b).
27. 256 U.S. 135 (1921).
28. 291 U.S. 502 (1934); 300 U.S. 379, 398 (1937).
29. 304 U.S. 144 (1938).
30. 163 U.S. 537, 559 (1896). Finkelman (2014a) argues that deference to the legislature was not the reason for the court's upholding segregation statutes in *Plessy* and other cases. Rather, he views the court as actively supporting segregation and perhaps willfully misreading the history of the 14th Amendment.
31. 372 U.S. 726 (1963).
32. 368 U.S. 157, 178 (1961). Finkelman (2014b, 1082ff.) offers a detailed and compassionate view of what life was life for blacks in Louisiana at the time of the *Garner* decision.
33. 381 U.S. 479, 511 (1965).
34. 438 U.S. 59 (1978), Price–Anderson Act, 42 U.S.C. §2210 et seq., Ely (2012).

35. 505 U.S. 1003, 1068–9 (1992), S.C. Code Ann. § 48-39-250 et seq.
36. 132 S.C. 2566, 2579 (2012).
37. 531 U.S.98 (2000).
38. 570 U.S. 12 (2013), 570 U.S. 2 (2013), Pub. Law 104–99, 42 U.S.C. §§1973–1973aa-6, as amended (most recently in 2006). In *Windsor*, the court determined that section 3 of the law violated the due process and equal protection provisions of the Fifth Amendment. *Shelby* refers mostly to the Tenth and Fifteenth Amendments but does mention the Fourteenth as well in note 1.

References

Books, Chapters, Journal Articles, and Databases

Ander, O. Fritiof. 1934. "The Immigrant Church and the Patrons of Husbandry." *Agricultural History* 8:155–68.

Anfinson, John. 2003. "River of History: A Historic Resources Study of the Mississippi National River and Recreation Area." St. Paul: US Army Corps of Engineers, St. Paul District.

Arnold, Thurman. 1967. "The Antitrust Laws and the Sherman Act." In *Legal and Economic Influence of the Grange, 1867–1967,* 1–9. Washington, DC: National Grange.

Arthur, Maude, Elizabeth Arthur, A. B. Hamilton, Lottie York, and others. 1951. *Heap O' Joy Grange Lecturers' Book and Booster Night Programs.* Syracuse, NY: Willis N. Bugbee.

Barns, William. 1967. "Oliver Hudson Kelley and the Genesis of the Grange: A Reappraisal." *Agricultural History* 41:229–42.

Baum, Dale, and Robert Calvert. 1989. "Texas Patrons of Husbandry: Geography, Social Contexts, and Voting Behavior." *Agricultural History* 63:36–55.

Boden, Robert. 1971. "Railroads and the Granger Laws." *Marquette Law Review* 54:251–53.

Bourne (Wahl), Jenny. 2010. "Give Lincoln Credit: How Paying for the Civil War Transformed the US Financial System." *Albany Government Law Review* 3:701–40.

———. 2011. "*Dred,* Panic, War: How a Slave Case Triggered Financial Crisis and Civil Disunion." In *Congress and the Crisis of the 1850s,* ed. Paul Finkelman and Donald Kennon, 159–202. Athens: Ohio University Press.

Bourne, Jenny. 2013. "To Slip the Surly Bonds of State Rights and Form a More Perfect (Financial) Union: One Legacy of the 37th Congress." Presented at the US Capitol Historical Society, Washington, DC, May.

Bowman, John, and Richard Keehn. 1974. "Agricultural Terms of Trade in Four Midwestern States." *Journal of Economic History* 34:592–609.

Buck, Solon. [1913] 1963. *The Granger Movement: A Study of Agricultural Organization and Its Political, Economic, and Social Manifestations, 1870–1880.* Lincoln: University of Nebraska Press.

Calvert, Robert. 1977. "A. J. Rose and the Granger Concept of Reform." *Agricultural History* 51:181–96.

Carter, Susan, Scott Gartner, Michael Haines, Alan Olmstead, Richard Sutch, and Gavin Wright, eds. 2006. *Historical Statistics of the United States, Earliest Times to the Present: Millennial Edition.* New York: Cambridge University Press, http://dx.doi.org/10.1017/ISBN-9780511132971.A.ESS.01.
Catalog of Grange Supplies. 1928. Syracuse, NY: Chas. Bainbridge.
Cerny, George. 1963. "Cooperation in the Midwest in the Granger Era, 1869–75." *Agricultural History* 37:187–205.
Coase, Ronald. 1960. "The Problem of Social Cost." *Journal of Law and Economics* 3:1–44.
———. 1974. "The Lighthouse in Economics." *Journal of Law and Economics* 17:355–76.
Coates, Dennis, and Brad Humphreys. 2008. "Do Economists Reach a Conclusion for Sports Franchises, Stadiums, and Mega-Events?" *Economics Journal Watch* 5:294–315.
Crawford, Harriet. 1939. "Grange Attitudes in Washington, 1889–1896." *Pacific Northwest Quarterly* 30:243–74.
Davis, Granville. 1945. "The Granger Movement in Arkansas." *Arkansas Historical Quarterly* 4:340–52.
Detrick, Charles. 1903. "The Effects of the Granger Acts." *Journal of Political Economy* 11:237–56.
Donnelly, Ignatius. 1873. *Facts for the Granges.* St. Paul, Minnesota: Ignatius Donnelly Library Pamphlet Collection.
Drobak, John. 1985. "From Turnpike to Nuclear Power: The Constitutional Limits on Utility Rate Regulation." *Boston University Law Review* 65:65–125.
Dupré, Ruth. 1999. "'If It's Yellow, It Must Be Butter:' Margarine Regulation in North America Since 1886." *Journal of Economic History* 59:353–71.
Dyson, Lowell. 1986. *Farmers' Organizations.* New York: Greenwood Press.
Ely, James, Jr. 2012. "Due Process Clause." In *The Heritage Guide to the Constitution.* Washington, DC: Heritage Foundation. http://www.heritage.org/constitution/#!/amendments/14/essays/170/due-process-clause.
Falck, William. 1967. "The Impact and Significance of the Granger Legislation on the Laws of the United States from a Case Law Standpoint." In *Legal and Economic Influence of the Grange, 1867–1967,* 57–82. Washington, DC: National Grange.
Fama, Eugene. 1976. *Foundations of Finance.* New York: Basic Books.
Ferguson, James. 1942. "The Grange and Farmer Education in Mississippi." *Journal of Southern History* 8:497–512.
Ferry, Darren. 2004. "Severing the Connections in a Complex Community: The Grange, the Patrons of Industry, and the Construction/Contestation of a Late 19th-Century Agrarian Identity in Ontario." *Labour* 54:9–47.
Field, Bruce. 1998. *Harvest of Dissent: The National Farmers Union and the Early Cold War.* Lawrence: University of Kansas Press.

Finkelman, Paul. 2014a. "Original Intent and the Fourteenth Amendment: Into the Black Hole of Constitutional Law." *Chicago-Kent Law Review* 89:1019–63.

———. 2014b. "The Long Road to Dignity: The Wrong of Segregation and What the Civil Rights Act of 1964 Had to Change." *Louisiana State University Law Review* 74:1039–94.

Fishlow, Albert. 1965. *American Railroads and the Transformation of the Antebellum Economy.* New York: Cambridge University Press.

Florida. 1881. *General Acts and Resolutions Adopted by the Legislature of Florida.*

Fogel, Robert. 1964. *Railroads and Economic Growth.* Baltimore: Johns Hopkins University Press.

Foster, Florence. 1894. "The Grange and the Co-Operative Enterprises in New England." *Annals of the American Academy of Political and Social Science* 4:102–9.

Franklin, John Hope. 1970. "Public Welfare in the South during the Reconstruction Era, 1865–80." *Social Science Review* 44:379–92.

Garwood, Saunders. 1968. "Florida State Grange." *Florida Historical Quarterly* 47:165–79.

Gilman, Rhoda, and Patricia Smith. 1967. "Oliver Hudson Kelley, Minnesota Pioneer, 1849–1868." *Minnesota History* 40:330–38.

Gustin, M. E. 1875. *An Exposé of the Grangers.* Dayton, OH: Christian Publishing Association.

Hacker, J. David. 2011. "A Census-Based Count of the Civil War Dead." *Civil War History* 57:307–48.

Hale, Lord Chief Justice Matthew. [1670] 1787. "De Portibus Maris." In *A Collection of Tracts Relative to the Law of England*, ed. Francis Hargrave, 79. London: Francis Hargrave.

Hart, Albert. 1887. "The Disposition of Our Public Lands." *Quarterly Journal of Economics* 1:169–83.

Hartman, Dorothy. 2013. "Order of the Patrons of Husbandry—The Grange." http://www.connerprairie.org/Learn-And-Do/Indiana-History/America-1860–1900/Grange-Movement.aspx.

Hirsch, Arthur. 1929. "Efforts of the Grange in the Middle West to Control the Price of Farm Machinery, 1870–80." *Mississippi Valley Historical Review* 15:473–96.

Hull, I. H. 1937. "Farm Purchasing Cooperatives." *Annals of the American Academy of Political and Social Science* 191:103–8.

Johnson, Emory. 1908. "The Trend of Governmental Regulation of Railroads." *Annals of the American Academy of Political and Social Science* 32:120–24.

Johnston, Louis, and Samuel Williamson. 2012. "What Was the US GDP Then?" *MeasuringWorth.* http://www.measuringworth.com/.

Johnston, Daniel. 1904. *Minnesota Journalism in the Territorial Period.* St. Paul: Minnesota Historical Society. http://archive.org/stream/minnesotajournaloojohnrich/minnesotajournaloojohnrich_djvu.txt.

Kanazawa, Mark, and Roger Noll. 1994. "The Origins of State Railroad Regulation: The Illinois Constitution of 1870." In *The Regulated Economy: A Historical Approach to Political Economy*, ed. Claudia Goldin and Gary Libecap, 13–54. Chicago: University of Chicago Press.

Keillor, Steven. 2000. *Cooperative Commonwealth: Co-ops in Rural Minnesota, 1859–1939*. St. Paul: Minnesota Historical Society Press.

Ketcham, Sallie. 2014. *Laura Ingalls Wilder: American Writer on the Prairie*. New York: Routledge.

Kile, Orville. 1948. *The Farm Bureau through Three Decades*. Baltimore: Waverly Press.

Klement, Frank. 1952. "Middle Western Copperheadism and the Genesis of the Granger Movement." *Mississippi Valley Historical Review* 38:679–94.

———. 1960. *The Copperheads in the Middle West*. Chicago: University of Chicago Press.

Kolko, Gabriel. 1965. *Railroads and Regulation: 1877–1916*. Princeton: Princeton University Press.

Kutler, Stanley. 1971. *Privilege and Creative Destruction: The Charles River Bridge Case*. Philadelphia: Lippincott.

Legislative Manual. 1874. Township and Railroad Map of Minnesota. http://memory.loc.gov/cgi-bin/map_item.pl.

Levy, Leonard. 1957. *The Law of the Commonwealth and Chief Justice Shaw*. Cambridge, MA: Harvard University Press.

Long, E. B. 1985. *The Civil War Day by Day: An Almanac*. New York: Da Capo Press.

McAfee, Ward. 1968. "Local Interests and Railroad Regulation in California during the Granger Decade." *Pacific Historical Review* 37:51–66.

McCraw, Thomas. 1975. "Regulation in America: A Review Article." *Business History Review* 49:159–83.

McMath, Robert. 1975. *Populist Vanguard: A History of the Southern Farmers' Alliance*. Chapel Hill: University of North Carolina Press.

Marti, Donald. 1982. "Woman's Work in the Grange: Mary Ann Mayo of Michigan, 1882–1903." *Agricultural History* 56:439–52.

———. 1984. "Sisters of the Grange: Rural Feminism in the Late Nineteenth Century." *Agricultural History* 58:247–61.

Martin, Albro. 1974. "The Troubled Subject of Railroad Regulation in the Gilded Age—A Reappraisal." *Journal of American History* 61:339–71.

Martin, Thomas. 2009. "With a Bang, Not a Whimper." http://climate.umn.edu/pdf/mn_winter_1887-1888.pdf.

Menard, Claude, and Michel Ghertman, eds. 2010. *Regulation, Deregulation, Reregulation: Institutional Perspectives*. New York: Edward Elgar.

Merk, Frederick. 1949. "Eastern Antecedents of the Grangers." *Agricultural History* 23:1–8.

Miles, John, Jr. 1967a. "Constitutional Impact of the Granger Cases." In *Legal and Economic Influence of the Grange, 1867–1967*, 17–35. Washington, DC: National Grange.

———. 1967b. "Impact of Granger Movement on Social Legislation." In *Legal and Economic Influence of the Grange, 1867–1967*, 10–16. Washington, DC: National Grange

Miller, George. 1954. "Origins of the Iowa Granger Law." *Mississippi Valley Historical Review* 40:657–80.

———. 1971. *Railroads and the Granger Laws*. Madison: University of Wisconsin Press.

Minnehaha Grange No. 398: Centennial History, 1873–1973. 1973. Edina, Minnesota: Minnehaha Grange No. 398.

Mixon, Scott. 2008. "The Crisis of 1873: Perspectives from Multiple Asset Classes." *Journal of Economic History* 68:722–57.

Naftalin, Arthur. 1956. "The Tradition of Protest and the Roots of the Farmer-Labor Party." *Minnesota History* 35:53–63.

National Grange. 2012. *Digest of Laws of the Order of the Patrons of Husbandry*. http://www.pagrange.org/Files/Admin/PDFs/National-Digest2012.pdf.

Olson, Mancur. 1965. *The Logic of Collective Action: Public Goods and The Theory of Groups*. Cambridge, MA: Harvard University Press.

Partin, Robert. 1957. "Black's Bend Grange, 1873–77: A Case Study of a Subordinate Grange of the Deep South." *Agricultural History* 31:49–59.

Paul, Rodman. 1958. "The Great California Grain War: The Grangers Challenge the Wheat King." *Pacific Historical Review* 27:331–49.

Pigou, Arthur. [1920] 1932. *The Economics of Welfare*. New York: Macmillan.

Prescott, Gerald. 1970. "Wisconsin Farm Leaders in the Gilded Age." *Agricultural History* 44:183–99.

———. 1977. "Farm Gentry vs. the Grangers: Conflict in Rural America." *California Historical Quarterly* 56:328–45.

Putnam, Robert. 2000. *Bowling Alone: The Collapse and Revival of American Community*. New York: Simon and Schuster.

Ransom, Roger, and Richard Sutch. 1977. *One Kind of Freedom: The Economic Consequences of Emancipation*. New York: Cambridge University Press.

Ready Reference Handbook of Worchester Made Products for Manufacturers, Importers and Exporters, Wholesalers and Jobbers. 1914. Worcester, MA: Worcester Chamber of Commerce.

Ridge, Martin. 1956. "Ignatius Donnelly and the Granger Movement in Minnesota." *Mississippi Valley Historical Review* 42:693–709.

Rose-Ackerman, Susan. 1990. "Deregulation and Reregulation: Rhetoric and Reality." *Faculty Scholarship Series*. Paper 597. http://digitalcommons.law.yale.edu/fss_papers/597.

Rosenbloom, Joshua, and Gregory Stutes. 2005. "Re-examining the Distribution of Wealth in 1870." National Bureau of Economic Research Working Paper 11482.

Rothstein, Morton. 1988. "Farmer Movements and Organizations: Numbers, Gains, Losses." *Agricultural History* 62:161–81.

Saloutos, Theodore. 1948. "The Agriculture Problem and Nineteenth-Century Industrialism." *Agricultural History* 22:156–74.

———. 1953. "The Grange in the South, 1870–77." *Journal of Southern History* 19:473–87.

Scheiber, Harry. 1971. "Public Policy, Constitutional Principle, and the Granger Laws: A Revised Historical Perspective." *Stanford Law Review* 23:1029–37.

Schell, Herbert. 1936. "The Grange and the Credit Problem in Dakota Territory." *Agricultural History* 10:59–83.

Schwantes, Carlos. 1985. "Farmer-Labor Insurgency in Washington State." *Pacific Northwest Quarterly* 76:2–11.

Sigmund, Elwin. 1953. "The Granger Cases: 1877 or 1876?" *American Historical Review* 58:571–74.

Smalley, Harrison. 1906. "Railroad Rate Control in Its Legal Aspects: A Study of the Effect of Judicial Decisions upon Public Regulation of Railroad Rates. *Publications of the American Economic Association*, 3rd ser., 7:4–24.

Smedley, A. B. 1873. *The Patrons' Monitor.* Dubuque, IA: Palmer, Winall & Co.

Smith, Jean Edward. 2001. *Grant.* New York: Simon & Schuster.

Smith, Ralph. 1939. "The Grange Movement in Texas, 1873–1900." *Southwestern Historical Quarterly* 42:297–315.

Soltow, Lee. 1975. *Men and Wealth in the United States, 1850–1870.* New Haven: Yale University Press.

Stigler, George. 1971. "The Theory of Economic Regulation." *Bell Journal of Economics and Management Science* 2:3–21.

Strand, Alfred. 1967. "The Impact of the Grange Laws on US Laws." In *Legal and Economic Influence of the Grange, 1867–1967*, 83–98. Washington, DC: National Grange.

Sutch, Richard. 2006. "Saving, Capital and Wealth." In *Historical Statistics of the United States, Earliest Times to the Present: Millennial Edition*, ed. Susan Carter, Scott Gartner, Michael Haines, Alan Olmstead, Richard Sutch, and Gavin Wright, Chapter Cc. New York: Cambridge University Press, http://dx.doi.org/10.1017/ISBN-9780511132971.A.ESS.01.

Taylor, H. G. 1936. "Simplification of Railroad Regulation." *Annals of the American Academy of Political and Social Science* 187:49–56.

Tontz, Robert. 1964. "Memberships of General Farmers' Organizations, United States, 1874–1960." *Agricultural History* 38:143–56.

Treleven, Dale. 1969. "Railroads, Elevators, and Grain Dealers: The Genesis of Antimonopolism in Milwaukee." *Wisconsin Magazine of History* 52:205–22.

Vale, Vivian. 1966. "An Anglo-American Cooperative Project of the 1870s: The Mississippi Valley Trading Company." *Bulletin: British Association for American Studies*, new series, 12/13:42–60

Van Zandt, David. 1993. "The Lessons of the Lighthouse." *Journal of Legal Studies* 22:47–72.

Von Neumann, John, and Oskar Morgenstern. 1944. *Theory of Games and Economic Behavior.* Princeton: Princeton University Press.

Walker, S. C. 1893. "The Movement in the Northern States." *Publications of the American Economic Association* 8:62–74.

Wicker, Elmus. 2000. *Banking Panics of the Gilded Age.* New York: Cambridge University Press.

Woodman, Harold. 1962. "Chicago Businessmen and the 'Granger' Laws." *Agricultural History* 36:16–24.

Woods, Thomas. 1991. *Knights of the Plow: Oliver Kelley and the Origins of the Grange.* Ames: Iowa State University Press.

Wright, James. [1874] 1885. *Declaration of Purposes of the Patrons of Husbandry.* New York: J. N. Johnston.

Newspaper Articles and Periodicals

Adams, Charles Francis, Jr. 1875. "The Granger Movement." *North American Review*, April.

"Cause of the Failure of Jay Cooke & Co." 1874. *Philadelphia Evening Bulletin*, July 29.

"Causes of the Popular Disregard of Agriculture." 1875. *New Orleans Times*, August 29.

"Commercial and Financial." 1874. *New Orleans Times*, July 24.

"Diamond Cut Diamond." 1874. *Philadelphia Evening Bulletin*, July 13.

"Eastern Railroad Rates." 1874. *Philadelphia Evening Bulletin*, July 27.

"The Effect of the Granger Railroad Law." 1874. *Baltimore Sun*, July 22.

"Energy Adviser: Public Power Was Hard Won." 2012. *Columbian*, August 22.

"A Few Practical Ideas in Relation to the Patrons of Husbandry." 1874. *Georgia Weekly Telegraph* (Macon, GA), February 24.

"Forming a New Party." 1884. *Duluth (MN) Tribune*, March 21.

"The Grange Movement." 1886. *Chicago Daily Inter Ocean*, November 13.

"The Granger Influence." 1875. *Philadelphia Inquirer*, August 28.

"The Grangers of Arkansas." 1874. *Little Rock Daily Republican*, April 15.

"Grangers to Hold Meet in Scranton." 1911. *Philadelphia Inquirer*, November 26.

"The Grangers: Interview with Mr. Dudley W. Adams, Master of the National Grange." 1873. *New Orleans Daily Picayune*, October 3.

"The Granger's [sic] in Minnesota." 1874. *Pomeroy's Democrat* (New York), March 14.

"The Grangers Move for Direct Trade." 1874. *Georgia Weekly Telegraph* (Macon, GA), February 17.

"Granger's [sic] Results." 1874. *Baltimore Sun*, February 12.

"The Grangers and Their Organization." 1873. *Pomeroy's Democrat* (New York), April 26.

"Grangers and the Transportation and Financial Questions." 1874. *Baltimore Sun*, February 23.

"Grangers Will Fight Bond Issue." 1911. *Bellingham (WA) Herald*, September 29.

"The Granges." 1873. *New Orleans Daily Picayune*, July 13.

"Granges Go On Record against Rum Traffic." 1916. *Wilkes-Barre Times Leader,* February 25.
"The Great Granger Movement." 1874. *Philadelphia Evening Bulletin,* July 21.
"Master Granger Gave Address Last Night." 1911. *Aberdeen Weekly News,* June 22.
Matthews, Christopher. 2012. "Occupy 2.0." *Time,* December 3.
"Menace to the Grange." 1909. *Morning Oregonian* (Portland, OR), December 21.
"Menace Now Seen in Laws by People." 1910. *Morning Oregonian* (Portland, OR), May 11.
"A New Element of Social Science." 1874. *Philadelphia Evening Bulletin,* June 2.
"People's Rule Party is Launched: Grangers Start Movement to Force Old Parties." 1909. *Bellingham (WA) Herald,* April 8.
"Practical Politics." 1886. *Chicago Daily Inter Ocean,* November 4.
"The Presbyterian General Assembly." 1874. *Baltimore Sun,* June 2.
"Railroads and Grangers." 1874. *Hartford Daily Courant,* April 13.
"Rural High School Advocated by Master Jones of National Grange." 1900. *Grand Rapids (MI) Herald,* April 21.
"Social and Political." 1874. *Hartford Daily Courant,* June 4.
Susman, Tina, and Andrew Tangel. 2012. "Occupy Wall Street Marks 1st Anniversary with Marches, Party Hats." *Los Angeles Times,* Sept 17.
"The Supreme Court on the Granger Cases." 1877. *Chicago Inter Ocean,* March 3.
"The Three Links: An Odd Fellowship Between Vanderbilt, Gould, and Villard—How They Combine." 1883. *Duluth (MN) Tribune,* September 7.
"Union of Industries: A New Political Organization among the Farmers in Missouri." 1874. *Chicago Inter Ocean,* August 4.
Untitled. 1873. *Georgia Weekly Telegraph* (Macon, GA), August 19.
Untitled. 1873. *Philadelphia Inquirer,* October 30.
Untitled. 1874. *Georgia Weekly Telegraph* (Macon, GA), May 22.
Untitled. 1874. *Philadelphia Inquirer,* July 15.
Untitled. 1874. *Philadelphia Inquirer,* July 21.
Untitled. 1876. *Idaho Daily Avalanche* (Silver City, ID), March 18.
Untitled. 1878. *Wheeling Daily Register,* December 27.
"The Western Railroad Agitation." 1874. *Hartford Daily Courant,* July 7.
"Will Missouri Grangers Take Notice?" 1874. *Pomeroy's Democrat* (New York), July 25.
"The Wisconsin Railroad War." 1874. *Hartford Daily Courant,* May 5.
"Wisconsin Farmers and the Railroads." 1874. *Philadelphia Evening Bulletin,* June 19.

Minnehaha Grange No. 398 (Edina, Minn.) Records, 1873–1985, Minnesota Historical Society, St. Paul, Minnesota

Box 1: Minutes, December 9, 1873–January 21, 1950. 18 volumes.

Box 2: Minutes, February 4, 1950–September 9, 1978. 8 volumes.
Community service reports, 1971–77, 1985.
Corn states grange lecturers' conferences, 1952–63.

             Correspondence and related papers: undated and 1884–85, 1908.
             Correspondence and related papers: 1923–65, 1977. 5 folders.
Box 3:   Financial records, Dues account book, 1938–49.
             Historical and background information, undated and 1874,
                 1927–[ca.1976].
             Historical and background information, 1925–53. 2 volumes.
             Photographs.
Box 4:   Photographs.

Minnesota State Grange Records, 1868–1994, Minnesota Historical Society, St. Paul, Minnesota

Box 2:   Lists of subordinate granges in Minnesota, 1874, 1963.
             Historical and background information.
             Photographs.
Box 4:   Record book, 1881–1916.

Index

Page numbers in italics denote illustrations on those pages.

abolition of slavery, 6, 22, 26–27
Adams, Charles Francis, Jr., 41
Adams, Dudley, 29
Adkins et al. v. Children's Hospital, 101–2
Affordable Care Act. *See* Patient Protection and Affordable Care Act (2010)
African Americans: Grange and, 28–29; segregation, 33, 103, 104. *See also* abolition of slavery
Airline Deregulation Act (1978), 100
alcohol, prohibition of, 83–84, 118n35
American Economic Association, 19–20
American Farm Bureau Federation, 2–3, 55, 58, 60–61, 96
Anthony, Susan B., 83
Anti-Monopoly Party, 55, 96
Archer, Hildur, 14
Arkansas State Grange, 50

Baird, Sarah, 3, 14, 48, 79, 80, 83–84
Baltimore Sun (newspaper), 35, 40
Beachfront Management Act (South Carolina, 1988), 105
Beef Checkoff tax, 58–59
"Beef: It's What's for Dinner" campaign, 58
Beef Promotion and Research Act (1985), 59
Berea College v. Kentucky, 102
birth control, 104
Black, Hugo, 104, 105
Block v. Hirsh, 102
Board of Trade v. Olsen, 101
Bone, Homer T., 64
Bouck, William, 59–60
boycotts, 60
Bryan, William Jennings, 96
Bull, Annie, 14
Bull, James A., 69, *69*

Burton v. Clyne, 101
Bush v. Gore, 106
Buxton, Austin, 60

California Milk Processor Board, 58
California State Agricultural Society, 60
California State Grange, 86
Carnegie, Andrew, 7
Carrabelle and Thomasville Railroad Company, 1
centralized purchasing. *See under* cooperative endeavors
charitable service, commitment to, 87–89. *See also* community service, commitment to
Charles Wolff Packing Company v. Court of Industrial Relations of Kansas, 101
cheese factories, 47
Chicago, Milwaukee St. Paul Railway Company v. Minnesota, 43–44, 100
Chicago Inter Ocean (newspaper), 53, 55
Chinese laborers, 61
Chowen, W. S., 68–69
Christmas tree tax, 59
Civil War (1861–65): aftermath, 6–9, 93; financing during, 9
collective action, 2, 3, 94–96
collective bargaining, 60
Colored Farmers' National Alliance, 29
Communist Party, 60
community service, commitment to, 3, 6, 55–57, 58, 65, 87–89
community-sponsored agriculture (CSA), 115n38
conscription, 84
Constitution, Granger, 17, 29
consumer information, 84

133

cooperative endeavors, 18, 46–50, 93; failure of, 51–57, 95; insurance, 50, 63, 94; politics and, 45, 54–57; production, 52–54; public utility, 45, 63, 64–65, 94; purchasing, 46, 47, 48–50, 52; secret rituals and, 57; selling, 47, 49, 50; single commodity, 58–59, 96; successful, 57–61, 63, 106–7
Copperheads, 34, 35
Corn States Grange Lecturers conference, 85
Council of Laborers, 29
creameries, 47
Crédit Mobilier scandal, 6–7
Crescent Grange, 73
"Cross of Gold" speech (Bryan), 96
CSA. *See* community-sponsored agriculture

Declaration of Purposes, 5, 14, 18–19, 29–30, 31, 45, 54, 67, 93, 96, 107
Defense of Marriage Act (1996), 106
degrees, *16*, 16–17, 57, 70–71
Democratic-Farmer-Labor Party (DFL), 96
Donnelly, Ignatius, 23, 47, *47*, 55, 59, 96
Douglas, John, 34
Douglas, William O., 104
due process clause. *See* Fourteenth Amendment
Duke Power v. Carolina Environment Study Group, Inc., 104–5
Duluth Tribune (newspaper), 24, 55
Dyson, Lowell, 60

economic improvement, commitment to, 3, 6, 18–20, 28. *See also* cooperative endeavors
Edina Mill, 68, 70–71
education: agricultural, 61, 77–79; commitment to, 3, 55–57, 58, 67, 76–86, 94; consumer information, 84; funding, 79–80; general, 79–86; health and safety, 81–82, 88; on international topics, 82; literary and cultural, 82; rural, 78; of state legislature, 82–83; of women, 79
Emancipation era, 6

eminent domain, 73
environmental law, 105

Farley, Robert, 54
Farm Bill (2013), 59
Farm Bureau. *See* American Farm Bureau Federation
Farmer-Labor Party, 96
Farmers' Alliance, 2–3, 29, 55
farms and farmers: borrowing costs, 25–27; discontent, 7, 19–20; economic improvement for, 3, 6, 18–20, 28, 47–48; educational and moral improvement for, 28–29; farm prices, 20–22; farm value, 27–29; property values, 22; storing/shipping grain, 25; taxes, 23, 27; transportation costs, 22–25. *See also* cooperative endeavors
Faulkner, Edward H., 79
Federal Aid Highway Acts (1916, 1921), 99
Federal Motor Carrier Act (1935), 99
Federal Power Commission v. Hope Natural Gas, 100
Federal Reserve System, 61, 62
Ferguson v. Skrupa, 104
Field, Stephen, 38, 98
Fifth Amendment, 104–5
Folwell, William, 23
Fourteenth Amendment, 2, 32, 37, 97, 100, 103, 104–5
fracking, 86
fraternalism, commitment to, 3, 6, 66, 67, 89–92
Freedmen's Bureau, 6
Freemasonry. *See* Masonic Order
Friedlander, Isaac, 53
Fuller Regalia and Costume Company, 15

gambling, 85
Gancy, Charles, 89–90
Garner v. Louisiana, 104
gender equality, 2, 3, 12–14, 79, 94
Georgia Weekly Telegraph (newspaper), 25, 40
Gibbons v. Ogden, 39, 99
Giddings, Franklin, 20
Gilded Age, The (Twain/Warner), 7

Gilded-Age laws, 1, 42
Golden Sheaf certificates, 57, 70–71
gold standard, 7, 27
"Got Milk" campaign, 58
government corruption, 6–7
grain storage, 38–39
Grange. *See* National Grange; Patrons of Husbandry (Grange); State Granges
Grange Insurance Group, 63–64
Grange Insurance Services, Inc., 64
Grange Mutual Casualty Company, 64
Granger legislation, 2, 31–32, 35–44, 97–100; backlash against, 40–42; legacy of, 43–44, 100–107; short-term effectiveness, 42–43. See also *Munn. v. Illinois*
Grant, Ulysses S., 6–7
grasshopper plague, cartoon, 7
Great Railroad Strike of 1877, 32
Greenback Party, 2–3, 55, 59
Greenberg, Jack, 104
Griswold v. Connecticut, 104
Grosh, Aaron, 14
gun regulation, 85

Hall, Caroline Arabella, 2, 3, 14, 71
Harlan, John Marshall, 103
Harlan, John Marshall, II, 104
Hartford Daily Courant (newspaper), 36–37, 40, 45
harvester manufacture, 49, 52, 95
Hatch Act (1887), 61
Hepburn Act (1906), 43
Hogg, James S., 35
Holden v. Hardy, 102
Holmes, Oliver Wendell, Jr., 102
Homestead Act (1862), 6
Hoover, Herbert, 61
Howard, O. O., 6

ICC. *See* Interstate Commerce Commission
Idaho Daily Avalanche (newspaper), 51
Illinois State Grange, 55
Indiana State Grange, 83, 88–89
Industrial Institute and College for Women, 79
inequality, 7

initiation fees, 14
Interstate Commerce Act (1887), 43, 99–100
Interstate Commerce Commission (ICC), 43, 99–100
Interstate Highway System, 99
Iowa State Grange, 39, 49, 52, 95
Ireland, William, 9
Itasca, Minnesota, 8–9

Jay Cooke & Company, 9, 53
Johanns v. Livestock Marketing Association, 59
Johnson, Andrew, 5, 7
Jones, Aaron, 78
Journal of Home Economics, 80

Kelley, Oliver Hudson, *8;* background and employment, 8–9; on collective self-reliance, 45; contract controversy, 54; on degree work, 16–17, 57; on effects of war on agriculture, 5; farm, *11, 76, 78;* on farmers' economic status, 28, 93; on middlemen, 22; as Minnehaha Grange founder, 1–2, 3, 68; Northwood project, 9, 46; on state agents, 48; on stock watering, 23; on subordinate Granges, 10
Knights of Labor, 11, 93–94, 96

La Follette, Robert, 98
land-grant colleges, 61, 79
land grants to railroads, 23, 60–61, 98
leadership development, commitment to, 65
Lee, Robert E., 39
legislative activity: support for, 65, 67, 68, 82–83, 86; transportation law, 98–100
Little Rock Daily Republican (newspaper), 54–55
Lochner v. New York, 102
Lucas v. South Carolina Coastal Council, 105
Lundeen, Ernest, 80
Lyceum Society, 68

Marbury v. Madison, 100
Marshall, John, 33, 34

Marshall, Thurgood, 104
Masonic Order, 2, 8, 14–18, 50
Massachusetts State Grange, 88–89
Mayo, Mary Ann, 79
McConaughey, Matthew, 58
McCormick, Cyrus, 53, 94–95
membership, 9–10, 12, 50–51, 56, 61–66, 67, 70, 71, 72–73
Michigan State Grange, 62, 86
middlemen: advantages of, 46, 53, 94; disdain for, 2, 18, 45; fees charged by, 2, 22
Millam, George, 68, 70–71
Milwaukee and St. Paul Railroad, 38
minimum wage law, 101–2, 103
Minnehaha Grange (Minnesota No. 398), 3, *13*, *15*, 22, 30, 49–50, 62, 63, 64; Chowen as organizer, 68–69; community service, 87–89; education, role of, 76–86; finances, 72–76; fraternalism, 89–92; hall rental, 75–76; Kelley as founder, 1–2, 3, 68–69; membership, 70, 71, 72; overview, 68–73, 92; parade float, *89*
Minnesota Department of Agriculture, 9, 64–65, 94
Minnesota Department of Transportation, 73
Minnesota Rate Cases, 43–44, 100
Minnesota State Fair, Grange booth, *78*
Minnesota State Grange, 18, 39, 48, 51, 73, 80, 84, 85
Mississippi State Grange, 50, 78
Missouri State Grange, 39
Mitchell, Alexander, 38
Morning Oregonian (newspaper), 55
Morrill Act (1862), 61, 79
Motor Carrier Act (1980), 100
Muller v. Oregon, 102
Munn. v. Illinois, 2, 3–4, 37, 39, 43, 97–98, 105

National Cattlemen's Beef Association (NCBA), 58
National Christmas Tree Association, 59
National Farmers' Alliance, 59
National Farmers' Alliance and Industrial Union (NFAIU), 59

National Farmers' Union, 2–3, 55
National Farmers' Union (NFU), 59, 60
National Federation of Independent Business, et al. v. Sebelius, 105
National Grange, 10, 12, 18, 46, 54, 60, 63, 65, 80, 86–87
National Home Economics Association, 80
Native Americans, 87–88
natural resources, conservation of, 84, 86
NCBA. *See* National Cattlemen's Beef Association
Nebbia v. New York, 103
New Hampshire State Grange, 86
New Orleans Times-Picayune (newspaper), 29, 40, 46, 47
Newsom, Herschel, 68, 98–99, 100
New York State Grange, 86
NFAIU. *See* National Farmers' Alliance and Industrial Union
NFU. *See* National Farmers' Union
Nix v. Hedden, 27
North American Review (newspaper), 41
Northern Farmers' Alliance, 59
Northwood real estate venture, 9, 46

Occupy Wall Street protests, 4, 93–94, 96
Ohio State Grange, 64
Oleomargarine Act (1886), 83
Oliver Hudson Kelley Grange, 89
Oregon State Grange, 55, 64
Osborn, J. H., 42
Osborn, Joseph, 48
Osborn, William, 34

Panic of 1857, 23
Panic of 1873, 9, 27, 61
Parsons, George I., 11
Patient Protection and Affordable Care Act (2010), 4, 105
patriotism, 86, 91
Patrons of Husbandry (Grange): on African Americans, 28–29; cooperation/consolidation, 46–50; decline of, 2–3; founding of, 1–2, 5–6, 8–9; free-rider issue, 63; gender equality in, 2, 3; legacies, 3, 93–107; Masonic background, 2; Masonic overtones, 14–18; mem-

bership, 9–10, 12, 50–51, 56, 61–66, 67, 70, 71, 72–73; mismanagement, 45–46, 52–54; mission, 3; organizational structure, 9–12, 17; purposes, 5, 14, 18–19, 31, 45, 67, 93; religious stance, 29, 47; railroad legislation, 2, 31–32, 35–44; recruitment, 10–12; regional shifts, 50–51; subordinates, 10, 11–12, 25, 50. *See also* cooperative endeavors; National Grange; State Granges
Pennsylvania State Grange, 86
People's Party, 59, 96
Peterson, Collin, 86
Philadelphia Evening Bulletin (newspaper), 24, 42, 55
Philadelphia Inquirer (newspaper), 40–41
plantations, 22
Plessy v. Ferguson, 103
political advocacy, commitment to, 6, 18–19, 29–30
politics, role of, 54–57. *See also* specific political parties
Pomeroy's Democrat (newspaper), 18, 49, 55
Potter Law, 36–37, 38
Prescott, C. A., 48
price regulation, 103
Progressive Farmers of America, 60
Proprietors of the Charles River Bridge v. Proprietors of the Warren Bridge, 33–34, 37
property rights, 32, 38, 94, 97
public good(s), 31, 32–34
public interest, 2, 3, 32, 37, 97, 101–3

Railroad Revitalization and Regulatory Reform Act (1976), 100
railroads: anti-railroad sentiment, 34, 40; charters, 33; corruption, 6–7, 23; Granger legislation, 2, 31–32, 35–44, 98–100; land grants, 23, 60–61, 98; lobbyists, 42, 68; mileage after Civil War, 1; as monopoly, 1, 23, 24, 98; public funds for, 32–34; public subsidies, 24; racial segregation on, 103; regulation of, 2, 25, 31–32, 34, 35–44, 94, 98, 103, 111n40; short-haul vs. long-haul issue, 23–24; steam locomotive in Minnesota, *36;* taxes, 22, 30; transportation costs to farmers, 22–25
Reconstruction era, 6
regalia, *15,* 15–16
Richards, Ellen M., 80
ritual, use of, 17, 18, 57
Robertson, D. A., 10
Rochdale plan, 49, 52, 95
Rockefeller, John D., 7
Rolvaag, Ole, 14
Roosevelt, Franklin Delano, 84
Rose, A. J., 11
Ross, Edward, 19–20
rural electrification, 64
Ryan, Edward, 35

same-sex marriage, 106
San Francisco Evening Bulletin (newspaper), 41
Sauk Rapids Frontiersman (newspaper), 22
Saunders, William, 9
Schall, Thomas, 84
secrecy, 17–18, 57
segregation, 33, 103, 104
Shelby County v. Holder, 106
Sherman Act (1890), 4, 101
Shipstead, Henrik, 80, 84
slavery. *See* abolition of slavery
Smith, Angus, 38
social interaction, commitment to, 55–57, 58, 65–66
Southern Farmers' Alliance, 59
Stafford v. Wallace, 101
Staggers Rail Act (1980), 100
Stanford, Leland, 42
Stassen, Harold E., 71
State Granges, 10–12, 18, *26,* 48, 54, 61, 65–66, 86, 88–89. *See also* specific states
Stevens, John Paul, 105
Stone v. Wisconsin, 38
Story, Joseph, 34
St. Paul, Minnesota, 9
St. Paul Pioneer Press (newspaper), 9
strikes, 32, 60
Strong, William, 38
suffrage, 83

Index 137

Sunbeam Grange, 73
Supreme Court cases, 100–106. *See also* specific cases; specific justices
Taney, Roger B., 34
Tariff Act (1883), 27
tariff rates, 85
taxes, 22, 23, 30, 27, 58–59, 84
Taylor, W. R., 36
Tenth Amendment, 33
Texas State Grange, 50
Thompson, T. A., 11
transportation law, 98–100, 112n1
Trimble, John, 9
Trustees of Dartmouth College v. Woodward, 33, 34, 37
Twain, Mark, 7

Union Pacific Railroad, 6–7
University of Minnesota agricultural education, 79
U.S. Army Corps of Engineers, 39
U.S. v. Carolene Products, 103
U.S. v. Windsor, 106

Vanderbilt, Cornelius, 7
veterans, support for, 87
Voting Rights Act (1965), 106

Wabash, St. Louis, and Pacific Railroad v. Illinois, 43, 99
Waite, Morrison, 37, 97
Warner, Charles Dudley, 7
Washington State Grange, 59–60, 64, 86, 95
West, Francis, 38
West Coast Hotel v. Parrish, 103
Western Progressive Farmers, 60
Wilder, Laura Ingalls, 6
Willson, George, 72
Windom, William, 39
Wisconsin Agricultural Society, 58
Wisconsin Dairymen's Association, 58
Wisconsin Marine and Fire Insurance Company, 38
women: education of, 79; inclusion in Grange, 2, 3, 12–14, 73, 94; minimum wage law for, 101–2; suffrage, 83
Woodman, Jonathan, 67–68, 92
working hours laws, 102
Worthy Master: National, 67, 68, 70, 78, 98, 100; State, 9–10, 11, 14, 18, 48, 49, 59–60, 69, 79, 83

Youngdahl, Luther, 85

www.ingramcontent.com/pod-product-compliance
Lightning Source LLC
Chambersburg PA
CBHW020654300426
44112CB00007B/372